Eric's Story

Surviving a Son's Suicide

Eric's Story

Surviving a Son's Suicide

Sandra Underwood

Copyright © 2003 by Sandra Underwood.

Library of Congress Number:		2003095543
ISBN :	Hardcover	1-4134-2474-0
	Softcover	1-4134-2473-2

This book was printed in the United States of America.

To order additional copies of this book, contact:
Xlibris Corporation
1-888-795-4274
www.Xlibris.com
Orders@Xlibris.com
20766

for my beloved husband, Richard,
and for all the friends who helped me to survive.

CONTENTS

A SELECTION OF POEMS
for my son

CHAPTER ONE

That day my husband Dick and I had driven the two hours from our home in Clemson to Atlanta to his doctor's. It seemed to be just another summer day like any other in August in South Carolina and Georgia, hot and humid . . . close. Except Dick didn't have classes to meet that day, and I had taken the day off to ride with him.

My husband had taught English at the university in our small town for twenty-five years, and I was an administrator, director of strategic planning, there. That day it felt a bit like playing hooky, getting away, breaking up the routine, having lunch at a restaurant in Atlanta together. And, though the drive was long and we had covered that ground many times before, it always gave us a chance to chat and catch up on each other's news.

That night we had gone to bed early. By 1:30 a.m. we were both sleeping soundly when our Samoyed dog, Sasha, began barking loudly and running to the front door. I sat straight up in bed, startled. I could hear the loud banging of the brass knocker on our front door. As I headed to the living room pulling a robe around me and trying to quiet the dog, I felt disoriented. Who could be at the door at this hour? When I opened the door, the bright blue light of the patrol car flashed off and on lighting up the dark night, forcing my eyes open. Sasha continued her barking and jumping so I slipped outside and half closed the door behind me.

"Mrs. Underwood?" the policeman asked.

"Yes?"

He tore a page from a small spiral notebook and handed it to me saying, *"You need to call this number at the LAPD. Your son Eric shot himself. He's dead."*

This was the way in which we heard the news of our only child's death—news that would change our lives forever. Abruptly. Coldly. Matter-of-factly. I felt *I'd* been shot. Looking back, there was no good way to hear it. And, at the time, nothing registered anyway but the information itself. I vaguely remember going inside the house and beginning to scream. Later on, Dick told me that I'd kept rocking back and forth wailing, saying over and over and over again, *"Now we have nothing! Now we have NOTHING!"*

I have no memory of it. Mercifully, shock began immediately to envelop us in a cocoon of safety, to shield us from the onslaught of the terrible new reality that began for us on that awful day.

CHAPTER TWO

In disbelief and feeling numb, I dialed the number at the Los Angeles Police Department the policeman had given me and was switched to the female officer assigned to Eric's case.

"Please tell me . . . what happened?" I asked tearfully. The woman answered, *"We got a call about six in the evening yesterday from one of your son's neighbors at his apartment building. He had left an envelope with a note beside him in his car addressed to the police officers, so we knew it was a suicide, but the first thing we have to do whenever a gun is involved is put a tracer on it.*

"I have to tell you, Mrs. Underwood, when we learned that he had just picked up the gun at the shop that same day . . . well, that fits a pattern we've seen many, many times before. You see, California has a fourteen-day waiting period on the sale of guns. When Eric waited the two weeks and then picked it up and used it on the same day . . . that means he had had a plan, and he carried it out exactly as he intended to. Unfortunately, as I said, we see many, many cases like these, and when it happens this way, it usually means that if he hadn't been successful this time, he would have tried again until he was. The way he did it meant he didn't plan to fail. I'm sorry for your loss, but your son knew what he wanted to do, and he carried it out just as he'd planned it. That doesn't make it any easier to hear, I know, but it appears it's how he wanted it."

Tears streaming down my face, I cried out, *"We had no idea! We just had no idea anything was wrong at all!"*

"Yes, ma'am. Oh, yes, in his letter to us, he asked us to notify

you and his girlfriend and his boss. Let me give you the numbers he left us. You'll have to call them. We are only authorized to notify the parents or the next of kin."

I hung up, my heart heavy in my chest, and called Eric's girlfriend whom we'd never met or spoken to before as he'd known her in Los Angeles for only a few months; he lived across the country from us and we saw him only two or three times a year.

The minute she picked up the phone (in the middle of the night) she sobbed that she already knew. Eric had left a message on her answering machine that she said was puzzling to her when she had arrived home from work that evening. They had been taking an acting class together and rehearsing their scenes for the last several weeks together. In his message, Eric told her he'd sent a check for her remaining classes since he wouldn't be able to do their scenes together. She said they'd done a "showcase" the night before—a performance where the audience is mostly prospective agents, casting directors, and other theater people—and they were so happy with how well it had gone. So this message she didn't understand . . . yet there was something about his voice and flat tone that left her uneasy, so she asked her roommate to go with her over to Eric's apartment. When they arrived, she said, the ambulances and police cars were already there. She was just minutes too late! She sobbed into the phone, and I sat there with hot tears streaming down, still disbelieving the horror of what was slowly emerging as Eric's last day on earth. *"I told them who I was, but they still wouldn't let me near him,"* she sobbed.

Calling his boss, a woman my age, in her mid-fifties, who was very fond of Eric and counted him as a friend, was no easier. None of the calls I was to make in the next days were. They were almost easy, though, compared to what was to follow.

CHAPTER THREE

That night Dick could feel his blood pressure rising, and he wasn't feeling very well. So an old friend of ours in town, Dr. Bill Hunter, told us, when we called and explained to him what had happened, to come right over to his house and he'd check him over.

On the drive there, at about 2:45 A.M., I told Dick we would need to talk to our travel agent in the morning about flying immediately to Los Angeles. And, it occurred to me that I would need to write and send Eric's obituary so people in our community would know while we were gone. I asked Dick what he thought about adding, *"in lieu of flowers, memorials may be made to the Eric Michael Underwood Fund which will be given to suicide prevention centers in Los Angeles and South Carolina."* He agreed that would be a better idea than finding flowers delivered to our door when we were long gone to Los Angeles. It was hard to believe we were speaking of such things as obituaries and memorials and a funeral for our only child. *"I can't believe it. I just can't believe it,"* we would say over and over again then, and in the coming weeks and months.

As I write this now, years later, I *still* can't believe it's true. Eric is gone. Our beloved son is dead. How could that be true? How *could* it be true?

I went down to my office at the university the next day, a Saturday, to write the obituary and to pack up some things. My staff and I were to move our offices to another building on

Monday. Now, my two dear "Kathies," as I called them, my associate director, Kathy, and our administrative assistant, also Kathy, like daughters to me, would have to bear that burden alone. A huge undertaking for them, but there was no other choice for us now.

———————————————————————

Obituary

The Greenville (South Carolina) *News*, August 12, 1995

Eric M. Underwood, Clemson

Eric Michael Underwood, 27, of Los Angeles, formerly of Clemson, died August 10, 1995 in Los Angeles.

He was a transportation engineer, and actor, and was employed by Wilbur Smith Associates, Engineers, Architects, Planners in Los Angeles with headquarters in Columbia, South Carolina.

He was a member of the Screen Actors Guild (SAG) and the American Federation of Television of Radio Artists (AFTRA). He appeared with Tom Hanks as the mail call sergeant in the Paramount film *Forrest Gump* and on stage in *A Map of the World* at the Odyssey Theater in Los Angeles.

He was an honors graduate of Vanderbilt University in Nashville, Tennessee, where he had a double major in civil engineering and mathematics, a member of Chi Epsilon, the civil engineering honor fraternity, and on the Dean's List, with high honors. He was a 1986 honors graduate of Daniel High School in Clemson where he was a member of the track and football teams.

Born in Ann Arbor, Michigan, he was the beloved son of Richard and Sandra Underwood of Clemson. Also surviving are his grandparents, Von Underwood of Plymouth, Michigan; Delores Hayes Nowlin and Terry Nowlin of Athens, Michigan and Florida; and his aunt, uncle, and cousins, Janice and David Young and Benjamin, Brian, and Lindsey Young, all of Athens,

Michigan. He is predeceased by grandfathers Harold R. Underwood and Donald E. Hayes.

Memorials may be made to the Eric M. Underwood Life Affirmation Memorial, 106 Blue Ridge Drive, Clemson, South Carolina 29631, which will, in turn, be designated to support youth suicide prevention centers in Clemson and North Hollywood, California.

Following services in Los Angeles, a memorial service will also be scheduled sometime in late August in Clemson.

Forest Lawn Funeral Home
Glendale, California

———————————————————————

As it turned out, we weren't able to leave for Los Angeles until a couple of days later until Dick's blood pressure stabilized. Dr. Hunter wouldn't hear of it. And we certainly didn't want anything to happen to Dick now, too.

Making those initial phone calls to our family members and our closest friends . . . and Eric's . . . was a continuing piece of the nightmare. People began showing up at the house and our closest friends, thankfully, took over and thanked them for caring and told them we'd have to see them later. I was in no condition to go over and over the story with everyone who wanted to talk with us.

Besides, we didn't really *know* the story yet ourselves. All we knew was that it had happened and what little the policewoman was able to tell us. His boss told us she hadn't noticed anything out of the ordinary at all. Eric had just received a big promotion and they had moved their offices to Anaheim. He now had a corner office and was more isolated and not quite so visible as he'd been before. But they were pretty close so she usually talked to him several times each day. The only thing out of the ordinary that Thursday was that he had asked to get off a couple of hours early. (As we learned later, it was so he could go to the gun shop and pick up his gun on the day that the two weeks' waiting period was up.) Everyone in Eric's office, all his colleagues and friends, were very distraught and shocked by the news. No one had had any idea. No one.

Even before we left for Los Angeles, we talked to some of his friends . . . and his girlfriend again . . . in Los Angeles. His acting teacher told us, as his girlfriend had, about the great success in their scene together at the showcase the night before. They had received a big round of applause and a warm reception for their work. His acting coach said he had walked Eric and his girlfriend out to Eric's car and that the two of them seemed very happy, laughing and talking; they drove off smiling. He said he was glad that was his last memory of Eric. He also could not believe what had happened the very next day. No one could. We were to hear that same remark over and over again. No one had had any idea. Eric, as the acting coach said later, was doing the acting job of his life. He had let on to no one what he had planned. Obviously, he didn't want anyone to interfere or to stop him. It feels shocking just to write that! Shocking to know that he had felt so hopeless. But then, that's what suicide is: hopelessness. An inability to see anything good in the future. An inability to even imagine a future. Just pain. A terrible, desperate need to escape the excruciating pain of it.

We had worried about the fact that Eric was trying to do way too much. He had two careers and was being successful at both of them. In addition, he had a long, hour-and-a-half-to-two-hour commute to work and back every day . . . in the typically heavy traffic California is known for. He hated that, and if we were there visiting, we could see the toll that that alone had taken on him. Lots of pressure, anger, and frustration from sitting in traffic . . . or at other drivers' driving. The minute he came home to his apartment in North Hollywood in the San Fernando Valley each day, he'd put on his workout clothes and head out to the gym to work off the tension and frustrations, and to keep in shape.

Eric was over six feet four inches tall, muscular, and very handsome. Blondish brown hair and blue eyes. Great smile. His friends in "the business" (theater, film, television) told him he had "the look" which meant, I guess, he was attractive enough to get auditions and roles and, with hard work and enough perseverance, the potential to "make it" in the business. A very tough business. A very consuming business. We worried about that, too. He'd certainly never thought about acting when he was younger.

That all came about almost by accident after he'd moved out to Los Angeles in 1990 to take the engineering job. After living there a while, he was volunteering at The Odyssey Theater (a good way, he said, to meet girls) and began working on Saturdays for a woman who was directing children's theater. He moved from sound and lighting and stage work into other aspects, and she took a liking to him (as many people did). He'd told us that one Saturday when they were working together she'd asked him if he had ever thought about acting. He said he'd told her, "Well, no, but it might be fun to give it a try."

He took some acting classes and soon after he had some small roles in a couple of plays. When he was in *A Map of the World*, he sent us the *Los Angeles Times* review (excellent) together with the playbill with his listing—a nice paragraph about him "making his stage debut . . . . " We were *so* proud of him. It killed us not to live closer so we could see him perform on stage and share his excitement over his new-found passion for the art and craft of acting.

At his funeral service and on visits and on the phone, we were to learn to our great surprise after his death just *how much* his various acting coaches and fellow actors thought of his talents and potential.

When the funeral service ended at Forest Lawn in Glendale, Joel, the acting coach he'd spent a great deal of time with (the coach before his current one), came up to me in tears and gave me a videotape of one of Eric's auditions. He told me not to look at it right away as it would be too painful. It was a scene about a man's relationship with his mother and in it he was angry. But he wanted us to have it, he said, because I'd told him (on the phone when he called us in South Carolina after he'd heard the news) how sorry we were we had never had a chance to see him on stage. He wanted us to see how talented he really was. How natural.

Joel also said he still felt hesitant to tell us something else, too. That a day or so after Eric died, he had received a phone call from a director who asked him about *"that tall fellow you used to have in your acting class"* she'd seen perform one time. He knew she meant Eric. She wanted to cast him in a role for a television show (if I remember correctly, it may have been a movie) she was working on. She thought he'd be perfect. She was shocked when Joel told her that Eric had killed himself. Everyone was. Everyone lamented the tragic loss of someone with so much talent . . . the loss of someone everyone liked so much. No one could believe it. Least of all, us, his parents.

How could it be true? How *could* this be true? Impossible! Unbelievable. The questions and laments of suicide survivors everywhere. The most shocking news you'll ever hear. The sharpest, deepest, most searing pain you'll ever know.

CHAPTER FOUR

O ur best friends, the Steadmans and the Bryants, drove us to the airport for the flight(s) to Los Angeles. Again, if it weren't for the miraculous cocoon provided by the shock state that occurs, it would probably have been impossible to get through facing each new day with some new horror that awaited us. They say that losing a child, or more than one child, is the most terrible, most painful loss of all. It certainly was for us.

Statistics also show that going through such a loss results in divorce in surprising numbers. In fact, that was one of the first things I heard from someone at work when I returned: *"You'll need to watch out for your marriage; most end in divorce over this."* I was deeply offended and began to learn to accept that despite meaning well (most of the time), people often don't know how to talk to you about what has happened. In fact, Dick and I grew closer than ever in our long marriage (by then, thirty-three years).

I remember being very surprised, on that hour-long drive to the airport to go out to Los Angeles, at how angry I was. Having no real information at that point—and knowing very little about the depression usually preceding suicide —I had concluded that something must have happened between Eric's girlfriend and him and *that* had caused him some kind of terrible hurt that made him no longer wish to live. He had told us how enamored he was of her . . . that she was *"perfect,"* etc., etc. But because they hadn't known each other for very long and he had had several other girlfriends before her, we hadn't made too much of it yet.

Now, as I searched desperately to make sense of the whole thing, she made a convenient (though as I later learned, completely unfair and untrue) target for my anger. She had sounded sweet enough on the phone, but who *was* she? How could *anyone* be important enough to give up your life for? I did not understand. I could not comprehend it. Any of it. I sat fuming throughout the long hours of the flight.

During the long flight to Los Angeles, Dick and I talked about what to expect. He believed Eric had left us a note explaining what had driven him to do it. That we would find it in his apartment when we got there. I, on the other hand, didn't believe we would. Even now I'm not sure why that was . . . that I didn't believe it . . . but it probably was anger at Eric . . . for having given up his life. His precious life! How could he? How could he have done that? That was the beginning of a long, long learning process that came to teach me much about mental illness, clinical depression, and the causes of suicide.

When we arrived at his apartment, we were saddened and shocked to find yellow police tape around his door saying we could not enter until we contacted the police. We went somewhere and called them and they arrived and let us in. On entering the apartment, the first thing we saw was the empty gun box on his immaculate kitchen counter. And, a box of shells . . . with just one bullet missing. And the receipt for his purchase. All those encounters, even to this day, come back vividly . . . and sickeningly . . . as markers of the whole experience. The nightmare of it all.

The first thing we did was look around the apartment for a note to us. As I had suspected, there was none. Yet even I was surprised at this because Eric had always been a very thoughtful child and man. How could he do this and not tell us why? I felt even more miserable. All of it felt just unbearable. And, impossible. We had already racked our brains trying to remember if he'd given any clues that we could use to explain this to ourselves. The three of us had been very close. Or so we had thought. Now nothing seemed clear or real any more. Nothing one could depend on. The world had turned upside down. Shock, confusion, stupor. And, gut-wrenching pain. The deepest pain there is to bear and still remain alive. Or so it certainly seemed.

It was hard to be there now where he had lived, where we had shared so many wonderful times and memories with him. They kept flooding back at every turn. In every place. You could hear his voice, hear him laugh, see his smile, feel him close. Pain unlike anything I'd ever been able to imagine. Our sweet son. Gone. I can't believe it, I would say, over and over again. I just could not believe it. The business at hand gave us no choice: believe it. It happened. Your son killed himself. Oh my God! Oh my God! It *is* true! It must be true! Oh, God, no, no, don't let it be true! Please don't let it be true!

So many of us live our lives not fully understanding . . . or pushing aside . . . the inevitability of death. Safe in creating a belief system that allows little or no room for the experiences of pain and death. Who wants to think of that? I'll do that when I have to, not before.

Looking back now, nothing could have prepared us for this anyway. Even if I had had some knowledge of advanced psychology and was, say, a grief counselor. Like knowing God, the death of one's child must simply be *experienced* in order to believe it.

That first night in Los Angeles, I told Dick it would be impossible for me to sleep in Eric's bed. I'd have to try to sleep in the living room, on his couch. Not long after we'd gone to bed and I lay there thinking and searching and unable to escape my thoughts, I heard, quite distinctly, *"You best Mama." "You best Mama."* I was startled by how vivid and real it seemed, as though I had actually heard it! I sat for a while, stunned and pleased, and then burst into tears, realizing the cruel truth: my mind had been playing tricks on me. I heard what I wanted to hear. Even though that hadn't been in my thoughts at the time, that had to be the reason. I felt all the more miserable realizing this must be the beginning of the torture we would have to endure from now on. It was a loving thing that Eric used to say to me, deliberately saying "you" rather than "you're." Just a sweet little endearment . . . that had come back to haunt me.

How, Eric? How could you do this to yourself? I asked. And not even tell us why? What had we done to deserve that? I couldn't understand. It seemed so unlike him. So out of character. But then, what *did* I know of him . . . now that this had happened? The whole world . . . our lives . . . the ones that I thought I knew . . . seemed like something I'd made up. I felt like Alice in Wonderland, the disorientation was so great. Everything I thought I'd known and felt sure of was now in question. Here we were left with little more than endless questions. And the deepest pain it seemed possible to imagine, much less endure.

Lying there that first night, my nightgown saturated with tears, suddenly it came to me in a flash. Eric had *mailed* us a letter. Yes, that had to be it!

His new computer sat there, formidably, on his dining room table. I had no idea how to operate it, how even to turn it on. But I had to know. Suddenly, I just *knew* I was right. This computer held some answers. I *had* to find out. I sat there, all night long, trying to figure out Eric's password to allow me into his documents. I tried everything I could think of, and none of them worked. I was about to give up, and then it came to me. (I am a great believer that these are no mere coincidences, no accidents. The universe holds all the information there is. It offered the information I needed.) Eureka! It worked! There I found the letters he had written to us, to the LAPD, to his friends. And, his journal.

Later we learned from his landlady that she had seen him — just before he had gone out to his car and into the parking lot — putting some letters in the mailbox just before it happened. In his pain and confusion, he had mailed the four-page, typed letter to us explaining everything. He hadn't realized that about as soon as we heard we would get on an airplane and come there . . . leaving our mail to pass by us as we flew across the country to Los Angeles. Despite knowing the contents of the letter now, in the computer, the one he had actually mailed to us was very precious to me, so the first thing the next morning (having to wait because of the three-hour time difference), I called my neighbor across the street who had agreed to take in our mail and asked her to watch for it and hold it aside.

I remember calling her again the next day, from a pay phone while standing outside the Los Angeles Police Department in the glaring sun, to see if it had arrived there yet. I felt very anxious about it for some reason. I also remember feeling, often, how surreal this whole thing seemed. Here we were, for example, about to enter the coroner's office, and the coroner was the same man we had read and heard things about when he testified in the O.J. Simpson trial less than a year before. He and his office had been called incompetent, and they were the ones who now had our precious son! Had they cared for him? Was his body treated with respect? What if there was a mix-up? An endless number of torturous questions followed us around for years to come.

~ ~ ~

What we learned from his letter to us was that for years (unbeknownst to us) he had suffered from depression. That his first bout with it had come on during his senior year at Vanderbilt. That since then he had had three or four other bouts with it and that each time it had come back, "it came back worse." He emphasized that no one was to blame. That we definitely should not blame his girlfriend . . . not anyone. That it was solely his decision because he just couldn't endure the pain the depression caused him anymore.

"*I felt guilty,*" he said, "*because you were the best parents anyone could have, and I know that it appears that I have everything . . . I believe life is very precious . . . but when you get to where I am, no one can say anything to change your mind, even if you know what they say is true . . . I must have a chemical imbalance in my brain or something . . . this has been a constant struggle for me.*"

He was very apologetic for the hurt he knew it would cause us. "*But I know you will survive this,*" he said. He said he hoped we would still carry out our plans to move to California to live near him when we retired. He listed names and addresses and phone numbers of people he asked us to contact to let them know. The letter began by telling us he had intended to tell us all this on a videotape, but when he set up the camera and started to talk, the camera didn't work right, so he had had to write it instead. Dick and I agreed that a videotape would have almost destroyed us. As it was, the letter . . . no, the act, almost did.

~ ~ ~

We were very grateful that Eric's close friend from the engineering firm where they worked quickly showed up at Eric's apartment and took care of us over the next week and more. A handsome, kind, intelligent young man from Somalia, Ali had had a wonderful friendship with Eric. He was as baffled and saddened as we were about the whole thing. But in his light, gentle, thoughtful way of trying to care for us, he would offer stories and anecdotes and share their good times together, making us smile. He thought Eric was very funny and he'd share funny stories to show us why. Everyone thought Eric had a great, dry sense of humor. Just like his dad.

Driving in Los Angeles can be very tense and exhausting, and we were both exhausted enough as it was from our grief and our inability to sleep. Ali drove us to the Los Angeles Police Department, to the morgue, to the North Hollywood Police Station where they had Eric's gun, to the gun shop, to the funeral home. He dropped everything from his own schedule and just stayed with us the whole time. Helped us through it. I shall never be able to express enough our deep gratitude. He was like a son to us, like Eric's brother. He *was* Eric's brother.

Again, the body's coping mechanism —shock —allowed us to endure and get through those awful days. Naturally, our first concern was to claim Eric's body and get it transferred to the funeral home. It's a surreal feeling to walk around in the beauty and sunshine of California and out into the horrors awaiting us at the Los Angeles Police Department. I remember standing at the counter and having to fill out some papers first for his belongings: his wallet, sunglasses, class ring. We were told we could not see him there. We'd have to wait until we'd made arrangements with a funeral home first. By then it had been several days since he had died. We set out then to find a funeral home and after a couple of bad experiences, settled on Forest Lawn in Glendale where they seemed to know what they were doing and were sensitive to what we were going through.

The man assigned to us asked many questions and, while we were sitting there, called the LAPD to make the transfer arrangements. *"I'm calling,"* he said, *"to make arrangements for Eric Michael Underwood who died on August 10. Yes, I'll wait."* After several minutes, he put his hand over the receiver and said, *"They say they have no Eric Underwood there."* Shaken and upset, I fished around in my purse and found the claim check we'd signed for his belongings. I told him the number, and then they were able to identify having him there. My precious, wonderful son had become no more than a number! My stomach turned over and I felt increasingly anxious and a little panicky. I was also furious. The American way of dying. The horror of the whole thing felt all-consuming.

"How long did your son live in LA?" asked the funeral director. *"Five years."*

"Hmmm, well, then, given his age and the short amount of time he's been here, I believe all we'll need then is to reserve our smallest chapel for the service."

I sat there wondering privately whether anyone would even show up. How would they know? The people Eric had asked us to call were few. The man came back with the news that all the other chapels were already reserved and that we'd have to reserve the largest chapel after all. Mostly I felt numb, just hoping I could even get through it, much less worry about the details. He told us he would call us when they had received Eric's body, on transfer from the coroner's office.

He also asked our preference about burial . . . or cremation. The question felt shocking to me. I had no idea how to answer it. Dick said it was my decision. That felt huge . . . too big a responsibility. It was impossible to think straight. Eric, bless his heart, had said in his letter to us that he would leave those arrangements up to us. My husband and son left it to me to decide. I wanted to die rather than decide on such a thing. We asked for a few minutes and talked it out: burial in Los Angeles would be too far from us even though that was the place Eric had considered his home. He had said he would never leave California. Burial in South Carolina seemed wrong; we had been planning to leave in a short time and move to California when we retired. What to do? In the end (in a decision that haunted me mercilessly afterward), I decided we should have him cremated and bring him home with us. We selected a heavy bronze container as well as the casket he'd be placed in for the funeral. Impossible! I thought. How can this be happening? How can we even be talking about this? Oh God, my poor, dear son. Gone! How could it be true? Surely it isn't true! But task after task kept reality right there in our faces.

Next we had to go claim the gun. It was being held at the North Hollywood Police Station, near where Eric lived. Another nightmare. I felt disembodied, like a zombie, just going through the motions of all this. Only the revulsion and my stomach turning over reminded me it was real. We were led down a long corridor past pictures on the wall of a smiling Darryl Gates, the controversial Los Angeles Police Chief. We had to wedge ourselves through a maze of desks (just like in the movies, I thought to myself) where officers were talking on phones, or to people who'd been brought in . . . a very busy scene.

We were led to a back area with steel storage bins. A pleasant young man took out the gun and gave it to Dick. I wanted nothing to do with it. How outrageous that my son could just go and buy this weapon and end his life. It made no sense to me. What if he hadn't been able to get a gun? Would *that* have prevented him from doing it? Another of those unanswered, unanswerable questions that plague survivors of suicide for the remainder of their lives. I was surprised to hear the officer tell Dick that if we wanted to, we could take the gun on the plane with us when we flew back home, if we wanted to keep it. Keep it! What? *"I thought that is against the law,"* I said to him. *"Oh, I do it all the time. Chances are they won't bother you about it."* I doubted it. And, there was no way I would leave this thing where we could see it for any longer than necessary. *"Tell us of a gun shop where we can get rid of it,"* I said. *"We will* not *be keeping it."*

We drove to the place he told us. For some reason I went inside with Dick and Ali, Eric's friend. This must be the same sort of place Eric had gone to buy it in the first place, I thought. How I hated all of them and what they did for a living. I shuddered, looking around at the displays on the walls and in the gun cases. And mostly at all the people, including women, who were there, "shopping." Were any of them planning to kill themselves? I wondered. Again, it all had a surrealistic feeling to it. If it hadn't seemed so important to get rid of the gun my son had taken his precious life with, I would never have come to this place. The idea of even touching the gun was repulsive to me.

In his letter to the LAPD, Eric had asked them to please be sure the gun didn't get into the wrong hands . . . especially into any kids' hands. He could think such a thing through. The aftermath of his own death! Again, my stomach churned. We left the place, having sold the gun, and walked out into the glaring sunshine again. Surreal. Maybe this is a movie I saw once. Or I am dreaming. This can't be happening. Oh, God, please, don't let this be actually happening.

Often we would say to one another, for many months to come, *"I can't believe it. I still can't believe it."* In fact, to this day, I still think that now and then. That element of disbelief is a hard one to shake. Especially when one's whole reality for the fifty-three years prior to that event was so very different from the life we were living now. What was this? Some kind of cosmic punishment? For what? What had we done . . . what hadn't we done . . . to find it had all come to this?

My faith before this happened had been fairly strong. Although I no longer participated in organized religion (I'd been an active Presbyterian for many years beginning long before we were married), I had come . . . through my own explorations and study . . . to some conclusions of my own about my "higher power." Something along the lines of the "Perennial Philosophy" . . . that the main tenets of most of the world's great religions held some important, overlapping truths. I had long felt a mysterious and deep sense of connection to everything and everyone and remember writing about that in college, and privately, in some poetry. I felt quite strongly that the discoveries of quantum physics and other new sciences such as chaos theory held great spiritual significance. I wasn't comfortable with "new age" beliefs exactly, but something much more sweeping . . . much less confining than any church dogma . . . seemed exactly right to me. Mostly, my spiritual beliefs had to do with my own experiences of the sacred. I suppose they'd come closest to mysticism. I had a great sense, since around 1980 or so, that we are in God as much as God is in us. As if we are part of the vast, living organism that is the whole sweeping cosmos. That it is through us that God learns what God is. Hard to explain exactly. But quite vividly real to me.

All exploded in the sound of a gunshot on a sunny day in August 1995. Well, (faith) lost for a while at least. Amid all the questions and confusion and anger and fear and sorrow. Awash in all the emotions. Funny, though, I never did ask, *"Why us?"* *"Why did this happen to us?"* Or, *"How could he do this to us?"* Obviously, he had done it to *himself*, not to us! I never believed he was lashing out at us. Though later some glimpses of those questions would surface and just as quickly vanish. It just wasn't Eric. He made it very clear how much he loved us. All his friends told us later how glowingly he'd talked about us. How supportive we had been of him. How close we were. No, it wasn't that.

What I had to do now was educate myself about depression. And, suicide. Clearly, I had a lot to learn.

CHAPTER FIVE

There was much to be done before the funeral. We needed to talk to the minister who had agreed to preside. And, to several of Eric's friends we had invited to speak.

Dick kept saying, each day, he couldn't believe what a great job I was doing, couldn't believe I was able to go on, doing all I was to get through it. He told everyone we'd see how proud of me he was. It was very touching and unusual for Dick to be speaking this way. Perhaps he had wondered how in the world we *would* ever get through it all and found real comfort in sharing the burden of those decisions and those painful days. Of course, it was, once again, the protection of the shock we were in that allowed us to go on functioning. And, we had to do these things. He was our son, our beloved, wonderful, brilliant son. He deserved only the best, the very best we could manage for him.

After having visited two funeral homes and leaving feeling dissatisfied, we settled on Forest Lawn in Glendale, California. When we first entered and drove onto the grounds, we looked at one another and smiled at how kitschy it felt —sort of like a Disney World for the dead and grieving. Carefully manicured lawns and grounds, lovely landscaping and flowers, several impressive mediaeval buildings, and old churches or chapels. A vast, gated complex, but one that seemed fittingly serious with respect to the magnitude of our loss and those of others who'd been memorialized here. The staff was extremely professional about everything and there were many, many small touches that provided the relief of feeling they knew what they were doing, at least.

When the day of the funeral came, I felt rather numb. I knew, or believed, I could get through it because I was little more than a robot by then . . . doing what I had to do. I had learned not to allow myself to actually think about what was taking place for more than a few moments at a time. Not allowing anything to "register" really, made doing it . . . getting through it . . . possible.

Dick and Ali and I entered the visitation rooms the night before the funeral, August 18, 1995. Eric's casket was there, blanketed by the most beautiful flowers I could select for him: star lilies, small yellow orchids, and greens draping the length of the casket—a gorgeous, fragrant display along with several others placed there from relatives and friends. There were two plant stands on which they'd placed Eric's photographs, one smiling and one serious, because, of course, the casket had had to be closed.

The first I had seen Eric since he died was when we had received word from the funeral home that they had received Eric's body from the coroner's office and we could come see him now if we wished. Both Dick and Ali asked in earnest that I not do this, but as I saw it, there was no choice. A mother needs to know that it is really her son, her child, there. That it wasn't all some terrible mistake after all. A necessary part of learning how to accept it, I guess. We entered the room together, and I looked only briefly. It was Eric, but not my warm, smiling, full-of-life Eric, rather, some distorted, cold, remote version, like bad art ruining the perfect, real-life version. Much later, I'd wished I hadn't allowed them to whisk me so quickly out of that room. I should have spent some sacred time with him on this, our first reunion since his death. I worried about that for a long while. Then finally—like so much else—I let it go. No choice. Too late. No going back. No way to go back and do it all again . . . differently. Any of it. Learning how to free myself from regrets and worries . . . if only's . . . took many years. (I'm still not there yet.)

Again, Dick and Ali and I entered that visitation room the evening before the funeral with sadness and dread.

As we sat there, Dick broke our silence, looking toward the casket with, *"Eric's dead. Where is he?"* A profound question, one that would be answered for me only after much searching over many years. I was very moved by the depth of my husband's grief as he voiced that question. Men deal with their grief so much differently than women do—part of the cultural indoctrination as males to preserve their tough exterior. Hard to do when your only child, your beloved son, is gone. Dick was so proud of his son, as we both were. He had often said, *"Eric has accomplished so much more already in his young life than I had even thought of when I was his age."* And, Eric had never given us any trouble his whole life. Other than a couple of accidents with his cars, he wasn't someone who was irresponsible or untrustworthy.

Eric had always been a happy child with so many different interests and talents that he was never restless or bored, always occupying himself with some new project or another. He especially loved to work with his hands.

Eric had just received a big promotion at his engineering firm in Los Angeles. He had become an engineer because he'd always enjoyed problem solving and was always building things or exploring new ideas and trying to make them real.

He had endless patience, even as a small boy, building intricate models, building and flying radio-controlled airplanes and even an intricate radio-controlled helicopter he had made himself.

Most boys love model trains. For Eric at around age ten, it had become a passion. He even built a whole elaborate city surrounding his train. One time I came home from a business trip and found he'd bought a huge board that extended from a table where he had the train to halfway over his bed . . . on which he'd added more to the city—a theater with real flashing lights on the marquee, a skating pond (a mirror) complete with snow and tiny ice skaters, stores and lights, and trees and grounds. It was terrific. I decided it would be *his* problem to figure out how to strip and re-make the bed from now on since he had to crawl in under the board to get in bed to sleep at night.

And, also when he was around ten or so he got a computer. By eleven or twelve he had created his own program for a video game he called Cliffhanger.

He and his friends would use our 8 mm movie camera to create stop/action films with some of the small figures from his city—whole stories and narratives (or "scripts") painstakingly moved slightly for each frame, to simulate motion. The finished films were amazing! One time he and a buddy had us howling with their movie about one of their teachers. Eric had "borrowed" an old wig I'd once had and one of them played/imitated their teacher in a classroom situation. Never a dull moment around Eric. I think it's the reason why he had so many friends. He was so inventive and so much fun. Always full of ideas.

Later, in his mid-twenties, his whole acting career had come as a real surprise to him, revealing a whole other artistic and creative side of himself he hadn't known was there. It was thrilling for me as his mother to hear him talk about it so enthusiastically as it unfolded. We talked every Sunday, but now the conversation might go on for hours as he would share his excitement about everything he was learning, the new people he was meeting, and all his experiences going out on auditions, meeting other actors, rehearsing scenes, or doing improvisations (which he'd been told he was particularly good at).

I remember the call we got late one night—a three-hour time difference with him in Los Angeles and us in South Carolina—after he'd been up all night long, all excited, following a meeting he had just had with an agent who had signed him on. Eric had only been taking acting classes for a very short time when this happened, almost by "accident." One of his classmates had asked him to go with her to read their scenes together as her audition for an agent. As it turned out, the agent liked Eric as well as he liked Eric's classmate and signed Eric on the spot. And, the man was a well-established agent who was expanding his business from a New York agency with lots of clients, so Eric was very, very fortunate because one of the hardest things of all to do for people in "the business" is, first, to find an agent to represent him. Many people spend years in Hollywood and still never find one to sign them on. All the feedback Eric was getting from people in the know was positive. He had a lot to look forward to—including several early successes. Yet here we sat, next to his casket. His life over. By his own hand. It made no sense. There was no way to grasp the enormity of it. The senselessness. It was, most certainly, a tragedy in the truest sense of the word.

So many people later on suggested to me that I must hold some anger toward him. "How could he *do* this to you?" they wondered. *That* made me angry. He didn't do this to *us*! He had done it to *himself*. How could I be angry with someone so loving, so caring, so wonderful all his life? I knew right from the time I finally read his letter that he'd been hurting. A lot. Suffering. In terrible, terrible pain. Sick. How can you be angry with someone who is sick and who needed help? It just seemed ignorant to me to think otherwise. And, insensitive. To even ask such a question. Or make such a comment.

However, as the months and years have gone by without him, there *have* been times when I have felt angry. Hadn't I *told* him we never expected him to be perfect? Why then couldn't he ask for help in those early stages . . . before it got so bad? Why didn't he go to a doctor? Did he really believe we'd love him any less if he were "mentally ill"? Apparently so. Mental illness, to this day, carries with it a terrible stigma in this society. And, perhaps he'd played out in his mind some sort of dire consequences in both his engineering and his acting careers if it were known he was treated by a "shrink." Perhaps he didn't have much faith they could help him anyway. I learned later that those who complete suicide often firmly believe their families, friends, and co-workers . . . the world . . . will be better off without them in their lives. That it would almost be doing them a favor to relieve them of the burden of worrying about them.

Before we left his apartment—as we were packing up his things before going back home—his boss, Kay, paid us a visit, and she and I sat and talked and cried at how wonderful he was and how much we missed him. How impossible—how "unbelievable"—it all still seemed to us.

Eric took great pride in his apartment. He had it nicely furnished and kept it clean and picked up. When we'd visit, he would pick up after us—especially the *Los Angeles Times* newspaper sections scattered here and there as we read. That's why it was so unusual, as I cleared out his things, to find a two-year-old *Reader's Digest* among his magazines. Then I discovered why—an article on depression and various treatments for it. His boss, Kay, is a woman my age, and she had taken Eric under her wing and had come to think of him as a good friend to her. When I showed her the magazine, she got angry (as I had earlier). It quickly became apparent that Eric had allowed that article to dissuade him from seeking help. It covered the stigmas involved as well as various treatments—all mostly long-term and taking many years and with some unwanted side effects, among them weight gain and impotence. And, they were costly. Eric made a good salary as an engineer, but Los Angeles, California, can be an expensive place to live, and his finances were always tight.

As most parents do, we had helped Eric with some of his expenses when he moved out there until he got on his feet. But he took great pride in being independent and doing well on his own, and he certainly wouldn't have wanted to ask us for money for psychiatric treatment and medication.

In fact, he hated medications of any kind anyway and prided himself on being healthy—working out, eating right, and not doing drugs or alcohol. He'd tried the latter in college and knew he'd have a problem handling it, so his friends later confirmed it for us—he wasn't doing drugs or drinking as is sometimes the case with suicides.

He was "just" clinically depressed. His journal confirmed it (when I finally figured out the password). *"I can hardly get out of bed in the morning. I have no interest in anything. No energy. Can't see anything good ahead."*

That's exactly what depression does, I would later learn through my self-education, research, and reading.

If one is treated early on for depression after the symptoms appear, it is easier to administer treatment successfully. If, on the other hand, weeks and months go by and the depression is allowed to deepen without getting any help, then the brain chemistry actually begins to change. The lack of serotonin makes it impossible for all the messages to cross the synapses in the brain. One can't think rationally or logically, and that is very hard for normal people to understand . . . or remember. There are heavy expectations implied in wondering aloud all the "whys." Expectations that could be met by people whose brains worked normally. But not by people whose thinking had become jumbled and confused. Recognizing this requires such subtlety that usually only trained professionals are able to identify what is going on at the time. By the time it has progressed this far, the only way a depressive *can* get better is to get outside help, usually a combination of psychotherapy and drugs, monitored and possibly changed according to the individual's needs and responses to them.

Without anything at all—no therapy, no medication, and increasing self-isolation and silence—life becomes flat and bleak, dark and hopeless. The struggle to keep going feels insurmountable. The pain is excruciating. You believe there is no way out but to put an end to it—to escape it. And, most believe they are not only doing for themselves all that can be done, but they believe they are doing their loved ones a favor, too. Relieving them of the responsibility of being around someone so hopeless, so much a problem, someone who is "mentally ill."

To our surprise, the visitation room that night (and then again the next morning before the funeral service) was becoming more and more filled with people who had known and loved or liked our precious son. It felt good to feel their arms around us and to hear how much they had thought of him, how shocked and sorry they were, how much they would miss him.

Because they needed several hours to transfer the casket over from the visitation rooms and building to The Little Church of the Flowers, where Eric's service would be held, we invited several of Eric's close friends to come with us out to lunch at a nearby restaurant. It seemed, like everything else, so strange to be here with them, talking and sharing stories, and not having Eric here with us, too. We were very glad we did that; everyone seemed to draw closer and share the pain with one another. It helped to deal with what had happened and to be able to talk about it among friends.

I had worried about how the minister, one we didn't know, might handle the fact of suicide. Many Christians and people of other faiths can be less than tolerant or comforting when it comes to death by suicide. Down through the years there has been some awful treatment to those who have died, as well as toward their surviving family members. Fortunately for us, the people we interacted with had, for the most part, become better informed by 1995, although there were, no doubt, censures and judgments that remained unspoken.

In his chambers, before the service began, the minister asked us if we had *"released him."* Worrying that the service he was about to perform in a few minutes might be affected by my answer, I looked at Dick and nodded, *"Released him? Oh, yes, released him. Yes."* As it had been little more than a week since Eric died, I thought privately what a stupid, insensitive, unrealistic question that really was. I understood what he meant, of course. But I also understood that this was a rather perfunctory part of his routine . . . the answer to which he could really have cared less . . . since he knew he'd never see any of us again.

While the minister did lapse a couple of times during the service into dogma suggesting the "sin" of suicide, for the most part he did fairly well, considering we were strangers and I had asked him to stick to the words and ideas found in the twenty-third Psalm, one of my favorites since childhood.

We were very moved to see the beautiful church completely filled with people for the service. We had had no idea Eric had even known that many people in the short five years he'd lived there. One of his best friends he'd grown up with, Todd, and his wife, Robin, flew in from Colorado to attend the service and to be with us. That had meant so much to us since so many of his California friends were not as familiar to us. Todd was like our second son. Though he lived only a block away, he had practically lived at our house as they grew up and played together. I flashed back to them standing out in our front yard by the beautiful blooming azaleas in their tuxedos with their lovely prom dates, and me snapping pictures and commenting how handsome . . . and beautiful . . . they all were.

As Dick and I moved to the front of the church and took our seats, I remember feeling very numb and disconnected, as if it were someone else doing this. The whole thing was completely overwhelming, and I doubt I could ever have made it through without my husband at my side. Who could have dreamed I would be attending my son's funeral and not the other way around? It made no sense. It defied the natural order of things. Dick's words kept coming back to me, *"Eric's dead. Where is he?"* I moved through it all as if in a daze, feeling determined not to break down completely and mar the solemnity of the ceremony. Dick seemed to be doing his best to hold up, too. The very idea of burying our young son seemed a horrifying impossibility to us both.

One of Eric's acting coaches, his dear friend, Kate, tears streaming down her face, gave some very moving remarks, commenting on the wonder of how successful he was in *two* full-time careers at the same time.

Here is what she had to say about Eric in a letter she had written to him . . . which she read . . . with tears streaming down her face the whole time . . . and then walked over and laid it at the foot of the casket when she was through:

"Dear Eric,

"I wish you would have stayed on here a while. Life without you will seem somehow incomplete. Where else in this sprawling megalopolis will I find a mannerly Southern gentleman to remind me that kindness and consideration can be a way of life?"

"You were always there for me—and for my friends. Every show. Every party. Every time I called you, you were there. I never heard you complain or burden anyone with the slightest hint of sadness or despair. Instead, you shared your endless energy, vigor, and determination at this thing called life.

"You had not one career, but two. I never heard you wince. Your creativity was bursting forth with no arena quite large enough to accommodate it. You just kept searching. When Hollywood's rejections came slapping you in the face, you sighed and turned the other cheek. To me, you were an inspiration as to how one can truly LIVE life. Not a moment seemed wasted.

"Tennessee Williams said that it's always the eyes that are the last memory we have of someone long since departed. D. W. Griffith said that the eyes are the windows to a person's soul. I guess that means that I will forever have a window to your soul.

"No matter what your beliefs are about an afterlife or reincarnation, there is one thing for certain. You will always live on in and through me. I rise to your challenge, dear friend, to endow the world with kindness, when anger and impatience would be easier; with consideration when laziness could go unnoticed; and with encouragement and support when selfishness might seductively come to call. You chose to love and embrace us. I can't help but feel that I've let you down.

"In your note you said to let you be free. It reminded me of an old Negro spiritual. I wondered if you'd heard it:

I wish, by golly, I could spread my wings and fly,

And free this always hurtin' heart that needs to rest a while.
To be like eagles when they ride above the wind,
And taste the sweetest taste of freedom for my soul.
Then I'd be free at last.
Free at last.
Thank God Almighty, I'd be
Free at Last.

"*I hope you're with the eagles and the angels and that you'll come down once in a while to fly among us and through us and in us. You're needed down here, ya know.*
"*God bless you and Love you and Receive you into his Holy Embrace.*

Love,
Kate"

We were also very moved that one of the vice-presidents from Eric's engineering firm made a special trip and flew in from San Francisco, having *requested* time to make some remarks about how much they had all thought of him, how much he had already accomplished at so young an age, and how hard the loss had been for everyone Eric had worked with.

Here's what he had to say about our beloved son:

"*I am very pleased to be here today because Eric is a very special person—very special to me, and as I can see, to everyone here also.*
"*I first met Eric in 1990. I think when we meet somebody, we all have, I think, certain clichés or things that we say, and I know I said to him, 'It's very nice to meet you'... or, 'It was a pleasure.' But I came away from that meeting thinking, 'Boy, it was really a pleasure to meet Eric.' I was really impressed by Eric.*
"*That first meeting was one where Eric had just joined our company in the Los Angeles office. I was on a business trip from San Francisco down to Los Angeles and I stopped by and just happened to meet him. I didn't know at that time that*

actually in a few months I would have supervisory responsibility over Eric and the other people in the Los Angeles office, and that particular responsibility was the time when I became close to Eric and got to know him. I took a step back the other day and looked into Eric's personnel file just to see what was in there, and one of the things I looked at was the résumé that he had sent and also a number of letters.

"One of the most outstanding things that I saw was Eric had sought a job with our company, going through our main office in the East Coast. They didn't have any positions at that time, but the word that came out through Personnel was, 'Look at this person's résumé. Look at the quality of this person. This is somebody we want to have in our company.' And, we went through the steps, and it was complex, but Eric became a member of our Los Angeles office. His résumé is extremely impressive, and when I summarize, I think you can see, as I say, what a special person Eric was. A person graduating from Vanderbilt University with a bachelor of science degree—a dual major, both civil engineering AND math—and I think what's impressive is that he did this in the four-year time frame. He also worked during that time. It's quite impressive that someone could accomplish that in just four years. And, he didn't just do a routine job of it. As I said, he graduated with honors.

"He received several awards . . . a Chi Epsilon award. He was a member of the national civil engineering honor fraternity. He was also named an Outstanding College Student of America, which meant he was in the top third of all the students in America. A number of different things, and while this was all going on, he was performing different jobs outside to help pay his way through college. Working for companies like Fluor Daniel . . . and a firm called Texidyne. Then also a job as a parking valet at a hotel . . . just to show the kind of diversity I think that Eric had in life. All these things, of course, I think, really appealed to all of us about Eric before we even met him.

"One of the things that I think is most interesting about

Eric is just thinking about what he did. His decision at that early stage of his life to move across the country—to move to Los Angeles—a place totally different, I believe, from any place that he'd been before. He made that big leap from the educational arena into the professional arena, and he did it with ease, extremely well. Which I think is quite impressive.

"About a year after that first meeting that I had with Eric I came back to the Los Angeles office to do what was, I think, one of the most difficult things that I had to do in my career. And, when I was given the promotion with the responsibility to take over that particular job, it was also made clear that because of financial reasons, that office would have to be closed. So, one of my first jobs was to take on that task.

"I looked at the people in that office and discussed it with other management people. And, we chose Eric as a person we did not want to lose. We wanted to keep Eric with the company. My trip to Los Angeles—the real reason for it—was to talk to Eric and talk to the other people in the office about the situation.

"As you can imagine, for anybody to hear this kind of news can be very devastating. Eric not only received the news well, he told me he thought we were doing the right thing. He said he definitely wanted to be part of the company. And, in the following weeks when there were a number of further actions that needed to be taken, Eric was always there. He was always supportive. He was suppressing rumors. He was doing positive things, and I came to really respect him for this high degree of maturity that he showed, but also the commitment that he showed.

"This, of course, left me with a very strong, lasting impression of Eric. Eric's work with the firm was just outstanding. It's something that has received special recognition. He moved up very rapidly. I think in the time that he was with our company he became a cornerstone of the operation. One of those people that everyone looks to and says, 'Not only is he somebody who's been with the company . . . but he's someone who you can look

to. You know that this person is a part of the company. He's a solid person.'

"We were all very interested in, and supportive of, Eric's interest in an acting career. Again, I think one of the amazing things about Eric was that he had this dual set of ambitions: He wanted to be the best engineer; he wanted to be a great actor. And, he didn't let the two things interfere with each other. He was doing both. And, quite successfully. And that is an amazing thing. It is something that we were all quite impressed by.

"I said at the beginning about my first meeting with Eric, just the very positive feelings that I had. I have to say that throughout the time I knew him, my respect for him grew. But also, I learned several things about him. I learned that he had a very good sense of judgment. That he, as I said, had a very strong dedication to what he was doing.

"But I think the thing that everybody got when they talked to Eric was that this was just one fine person. A person that is enjoyable to be dealing with and a person who is enjoyable to spend time with. A person who has very strong values. Somebody that we can all respect and look up to.

"So, I'd like to leave you with what I started with, really. That I'd just like to say:

"Eric, it's been a pleasure knowing you."

~ ~ ~

In addition, his boss, Kay, went out of her way to speak about all of Eric's strengths, talents, and endearing qualities. There wasn't a dry eye in the house, as they say. Here are her remarks:

"My friend, Eric! Ah, my mind is brimming with so many happy remembrances of you and your radiant life, and they are so very special to me. It is such a great honor for me to celebrate your life today before your family and friends, to share with them the excellence you achieved as a transportation engineer *and to speak of you, my affectionate friend. I am here today to celebrate your work as a consultant in the transportation field.*

"As a boss, it was personally rewarding for me to be a part of your growth, Eric, in a short time from being a junior-level transportation engineer at Wilbur Smith Associates to assuming the responsibility of project manager. We consultants know what a big deal it is to be a project manager and what a grind it can be! Of course, Eric, you were impressive in this role, meeting schedules, overseeing all aspects of the work, producing a quality product, making presentations, not getting too pissed off at clients' unreasonable demands, and bringing the jobs in on budget—the all important bottom line.

"But, what is the key to all of this success? Why, this is too easy, a real slamdunk, in fact—Eric, your outstanding personal qualities of honesty, integrity, responsibility, excellence, energy, and oh, lest I forget—intelligence.

"I was so happy to congratulate you recently on your professional accomplishment of being awarded a mid-year promotion at Wilbur Smith Associates in recognition of a job well done and for your overall contribution to the success of our office and the firm.

"But there is so much more to celebrate about you as a fellow employee for those of us who worked side by side with you every day. You were fun-loving and funny, too—in that very Eric ironic way of helping to lessen the tension of yet another deadline or questionable computer run with just the right witticism. Or, should I say 'King Eric!' Well, you weren't 'King of the Hoops' every week, but you were always a tough competitor for the office basketball championship. Your sensitivity in your personal relationships with all of us, always quick with a kindness and understanding, helped make our office environment rich in caring and team spirit.

"I am here today to celebrate you as a friend, Eric, my dear friend. I am here today to celebrate the joy of your friendship for your comrades at Wilbur Smith Associates: Bob, Guoxiong, Judy,

Minh, Barbara, Bill, and John in New Haven. You enriched all of our lives by your bright presence.

"I'm trying to recall how we grew from an obvious mixed-matched pair of boss and employee, middle-aged woman and youthful man, to share this friendship. Learning to trust one another was a long process, you with your reserve and me with my anxiety. I trusted you, my friend! It sounds so simple, but it is amazingly complex. Eric, I know you will understand when I say that friendship is a precious wonderment; however, speaking about friendship seems to border on the cliché.

"We both brought to our friendship a special shared intellect—you with your always bright, young mind and me with my layers of experience. What fun we enjoyed together listening to music, talking about absolutely everything contemporary, and the constant banter that stimulated our minds.

"But I'm here today to celebrate your sensitivity, warmth, support, understanding, caring, and fun as my friend. Tough days for me became easier, because you were near. Sharing joys became more joyous, because you were near. Life's dreams had more meaning, because you were near.

"And, there were many, many fun times! What fun we had together on our shopping excursion to purchase Bob's Singapore survival kit, dashing out of the office to grab some lunch, sharing videos and music tapes, and your always welcome quips and laughter. I loved taking you by the hand at my daughter Shannon's wedding reception in June and introducing you to my family and friends as my colleague, but more importantly, as my chum.

"And, you were such a comfortable and comforting friend. Always sweet, steadfast, and sensitive to my feelings when things were rocky either at work or in my personal life. The comfort you so generously offered gave me strength. I love you, my affectionate friend!"

~ ~ ~

Eric, we believe, would have been so very honored by all their remarks on that day.

After the service, Dick and I were led up to where the flower-draped coffin was, and a long stream of people began coming up to us to express their sorrow and condolences. It was just so hard to understand how someone that everyone clearly thought so much of could have felt so isolated, alone, and lost, to have taken his own life. One of the mysteries of suicide for the survivors is asking such questions over and over again throughout the years of their own remaining time on earth.

Following the funeral service, as people began leaving the chapel, we invited some of Eric's closest friends to join us at his favorite restaurant—one where he'd always take friends or a new date—a Greek restaurant with fabulous food and music and waiters in costume who would, at intervals, dance around the room ala Zorba the Greek. Very festive and always a lot of fun. A very happy feeling. We had been there with him a couple of times before. We joined together and made a toast in celebration of Eric's wonderful life. Just as he would have wanted us to do. To be together at a place he loved, keeping him with us, remembering the good times we had had with him.

CHAPTER SIX

Elizabeth Kubler Ross' pioneering work on death and the various stages of grief have helped in getting people to face death openly and to begin the process of moving toward healing. As I was to learn, though, the grieving process was neither so neat nor linear as one would have hoped after reading about each stage (that is, if I get through "anger," maybe now I'm finally ready to move on to "acceptance," for example). The unique fact of the means of death—self-inflicted—is what perhaps changes all that. Particularly when it's a young person.

We have always heard that it is the horror of all horrors for parents to lose a child. But losing a child (in Eric's case, a beloved *only* child) to suicide just deepens the horror and sense of loss and anguish.

Parents naturally blame themselves, each thinking, *"If only I'd done this . . . or that."* If only. Or, *"If I'd gone out there and was there with him this would never have happened."* Eventually, but only after many many months, or perhaps years, you realize (and come to respect in a new way) that he was an individual with a life of his own. Apart from us. His decision to end his life was his and his alone. And that, in fact, is what he was telling us in his letter to us.

One insight I experienced that helped me was realizing that when *I* was a young woman Eric's age, what ran through *my* mind about my life was hardly, first and foremost, what my *parents* thought of things or what *they* would do in a given situation. By then, I had my *own* life and my own ideas about everything. My problems and issues and worries and fantasies and dreams and hopes and loves and hates had, for the most part, nothing much to do with what my mother or father might think about them. Eric's thoughts likely surrounded his work, his friends, his girlfriend, acting—the world in which he lived now, not the world he had once inhabited as a child and the one in which parents often try to return even their adult children to.

Which wasn't so much an attempt to find a way to get us "off the hook," so to speak, but rather to be realistic about what may *really* have been in his mind during those awful weeks and months.

William Styron in *Darkness Visible: A Memoir of Madness* is one of the very best writers I know in describing what that darkness of depression feels like:

> *"My brain had begun to endure its familiar siege,"* Styron wrote. *"My thought processes were being engulfed by a toxic and unnameable tide that obliterated any enjoyable response to the living world. This is to say more specifically ... I was feeling in my mind a sensation close to, but indescribably different from, actual pain."* He told his daughter he *"would prefer to have his arm cut off without anesthesia than live with the agony in his head."*

In his case, Styron hospitalized himself because he *knew* he couldn't handle it on his own without help. When he recovered, he wrote his memoir, he said, when he *"found himself surrounded by ignorance of his illness and subjected to demeaning moralizing. I wrote the memoir in order to help abolish the stigma. I did it because I was enraged to discover that so many people did regard the illness as a moral defect or a character failure. It wasn't psychobabble or some need to strip myself naked. It was really a need that came out of anger, to put people straight that it was an illness and not a moral failing. I thought it was inconceivable that there would be a time I would be in good health. But eventually I was. I needed seven weeks in a hospital . . . ."*

William Styron and others talk about how strange it is to become aware of oneself watching and observing oneself. It's especially strange during those (or these) times of depression and deep sadness when everything feels "flat" anyway—one is a detached observer watching a detached observer . . . looking back!

These helped give me insights into what Eric was facing. What was in his mind. And, all the stigmas faced by people who are depressed . . . from those willing to talk about it. Many side effects have been mentioned from the drugs some people must use. And, even electric shock treatments were cited as helpful in cases where patients don't respond well to drugs.

William Styron says, correctly, that the word "depression" has come to mean almost nothing as related to the deeper, clinical depression that causes enough psychic pain to make people want to escape it by dying. They just want the pain to end. Not their lives. But Dick and I also know that Eric was a very sharp, very savvy fellow. And, as we said, we even found articles on depression . . . AND the costs . . . and side effects associated with the drugs one must take. To him those were unacceptable with his brain by then no longer functioning normally. He really saw no other way out of it. Or, at least he had convinced himself there was no other way. He didn't want to die. He wasn't angry with anyone, including himself. He just couldn't live with the pain he was in. He had to be free of it.

And, if later on *I* hadn't actually *felt* and lived with that same pain myself . . . that was to drive even me to make actual plans and get to the water's edge once . . . I *still* wouldn't be able to fully comprehend it. That's what Styron said, too. Unless you have actually experienced this kind of psychic pain yourself, then you *don't* . . . *can't* really know what it is like for them who complete suicide. Since I was spared carrying out my own plans, I can look back now and see my experience of all that as Eric's true gift to me as his mother, or else *I* would never, really, have understood, either. It really doesn't have anything to do with how you could *do* this to someone else . . . to those you would leave behind, like my dear, grieving husband. It has only to do with being unable to live with the pain, the excruciating pain you feel. You see no other way out. Not even therapy or drugs.

Often Dick and I realize, when we hear some horror stories of people who have tried to help severely depressed people who have to be hospitalized, some more than once or twice, only to go through that hell and then STILL lose them, that it could actually have been worse. Yet, we have both agreed countless times now that no matter how frustrating, how problematic, how costly, how seemingly *hopeless* the situation might really have been . . . including Eric's mental illness . . . still, we would heartily welcome having had the chance to try everything possible to have saved him.

Nine out of ten people CAN be saved. And, what would several years' pain and heartache and frustration be compared to a life without him . . . forever? Something very minor, to be sure. We haven't lived that, so perhaps we aren't really in a place to say. But we have lived this—for eight years now—and there is no doubt which we would choose. We'd move mountains trying to find some way . . . any way . . . to help him. No question about it. He was just that wonderful . . . and needed.

Often one hears, *"They had everything to live for,"* so why would they choose suicide? As Styron said, unless *you* have actually experienced what that pain is like, one can't know really. Which is what makes this problem so very tough, and why there is still so much stigma attached to it. How could someone who does have everything—when so many people in the world have so little—*be* so "selfish" and "self-absorbed" and "ungrateful" that they could give it all up AND hurt so many people they leave behind? How?

"Because all you know is, you MUST stop this pain," as Styron and others assure us. Eric had a dear and tender heart . . . and a lot of pride. He was very independent. He always wanted to take care of everything all by himself. And, that's what he thought he was doing. He couldn't *see* any other options because, by then,

his brain was unable to process anything else. My heart broke again, later on, when I found in the Daytimer he carried to work with him . . . in an old note he had scribbled on a great day, "*My life is a miracle.*"

It wasn't that he didn't value his life and all he had. It was that he thought (or so I've determined)—*"If I feel THIS bad, again, when I have everything going so well for me right now*—a big promotion on his engineering job, a beautiful girlfriend, fairly quick success with acting (an agent and already in the hit movie *Forrest Gump*, just practicing it after work hours on the side) . . . and auditions coming in to do national commercials and even new television series . . . a loving family, great friends, a beautiful apartment—*if I feel this bad when I have all the things anyone could ever want . . . and STILL I get this depressed, well then obviously I'll never be able to get this right . . . if, say, things were to go sour sometime later. So there MUST be something wrong with me . . . a character flaw or something that makes me weak and unable to cope with this. I can't do it anymore. I can't do this anymore. It hurts so much feeling this way. I just can't see living the rest of my life like this. There are no other options."*

Again, William Styron says it best, I think . . . and eloquently, that *"depression can be as serious a medical affair as diabetes or cancer"*—and that, as it progresses (if it is allowed to)—there comes a point at which nothing external anymore could be called *"the cause."* He says, correctly, that it is nearly impossible for an outsider (that is one who has NOT experienced the depths of this) to *"grasp the essence of the illness"* . . . or to KNOW what it *feels* like to the sufferer.

Styron says that *because* of this, the stigma continues and the person who completes the suicide is considered a disappointment, or has "*. . . demonstrated a frailty, a crumbling of character they were loath to accept . . . and a touch of shame . . . .*" And this makes Styron, like me, furious! As a result, he was moved to begin speaking openly about it.

"The pain of severe depression is quite unimaginable to those

who have not suffered it, and it kills in many instances because its anguish can no longer be borne. The prevention of many suicides will continue to be hindered until there is a general awareness of the nature of this pain. Through the healing process of time—and through medical intervention or hospitalization in many cases—most people survive depression, which may be its only blessing; but to the tragic legion who are compelled to destroy themselves there should be no more reproof attached than to the victims of terminal cancer."

There continues to be so much ignorance, stigma, insensitivity, and misunderstanding. There are too few people, still alive, who have actually *felt* the depths of that pain and know how it differs from ordinary bouts of depression. Those who didn't make it need a voice.

Kay Jamison's book, *Night Falls Fast: Understanding Suicide*—like William Styron's *Darkness Visible*—has the perspective of someone who has suffered from depression (in her case, manic depression) and has attempted suicide because of it. She also knows what she is talking about. Her book concentrates on suicides in those under forty. She's done a lot of research and has found that suicide has killed more young people in the last forty years than the total of those who died in the Vietnam War AND from HIV/AIDS.

> *"Suicide, by any reckoning, is a major killer of the young . . . . Wars come and go, epidemics come and go; but suicide, thus far, has stayed.*

> *"Suicide is a particularly awful way to die: the mental suffering leading up to it is usually prolonged, intense, and unpalliated. There is no morphine equivalent to ease the acute pain, and death not uncommonly is violent and grisly. The suffering of the suicidal is private and inexpressible, leaving family members,*

*friends, and colleagues to deal with an almost unfathomable
kind of loss, as well as guilt. Suicide carries in its aftermath a
level of confusion and devastation that is, for the most part,
beyond description. Most suicides, although by no means all,
can be prevented. The breach between what we know and do is
lethal."*

Styron, William. *Darkness Visible: A Memoir of Madness.* New York: Vintage Books, 1990.

Jamison, M.D., Kay Redfield. *Night Falls Fast: Understanding Suicide.* New York: Knopf, 1999.

CHAPTER SEVEN

After the funeral, our time was spent dismantling Eric's apartment and packing up his things and arranging with movers to ship everything back to South Carolina.

I remember standing in front of his bathroom mirror sobbing as I took down all the pictures and inspirational quotes he'd taped up there to see and to keep himself going. They'd worked for a while at least. It was just so touching how hard he'd been trying. Heartbreaking.

Near his bed on a shelf with his clock I found he'd kept several letters I had written to him—letters of praise and encouragement, of pride in him and his accomplishments—but also (to my relief at the time), assurances that failure was okay, too. Necessary, sometimes, to learn from it and to grow. That he never had to feel he must be "perfect." (Though, like many high achievers, he did tend to strive for that.) We would always love him more than anything. No matter what. At least I had said it. And, if I hadn't found those letters, I might have tormented myself still further than I already was doing. Those dogged "what ifs" and "if onlys" that plague those left behind. There are plenty enough of those just knowing how very imperfect we are as individuals and as his parents.

One of the things I was determined to do before leaving Los Angeles was to contact the closest suicide hotline/prevention center to determine where we might send half of our fund—to help them try to help others who need it.

After several phone calls, I became quite frustrated—not only with constant busy signals and runarounds (what, I couldn't help thinking, if I were Eric calling and needing help . . . NOW! . . . but couldn't get through and so, I just gave up!)

Finally, I found someone at the Family Service of Los Angeles who had a big, effective suicide prevention program that had been in service for many years. He outlined the work they do and, when I told him Eric's story, he told me of some heartbreaking cases they had had. After talking to him awhile, I was satisfied they could use our financial help and told him we would be sending a check sometime later after we returned home.

I remember, too, as I packed up his things, sort of automatically—as I'd done before when I'd stayed with him and he was working so hard—taking his laundry over to the laundry room in the apartment complex and washing it. It was only when it was already too late that I realized that in doing so, I'd given up traces of his scent, on his shirts, his pillow case, etc. Gone! More sobbing. More devastation. More loss. Of even something so fleeting as his scent. So precious to a grieving mother. I could have worn his shirt. I could have buried my face in his pillow and absorbed what little was left of him into my senses. Instead, robotically, I had reverted to the helpful mother, tidying up. And now, even that was lost.

We had the packing to do and things like closing up his accounts and advertising to sell his car, etc.

On August 10, 1995, at approximately 5:30 P.M. (PST), Eric dropped off his mail, waved to his landlady in her office near the mailboxes, just as he did every day, and walked out in his workout clothes carrying his sports bag as if on his way, as usual, to the gym. He got in his car in the parking lot behind the complex, in his assigned place by a small tree, reached in his gym bag, and pulled out the gun, carefully placing the letter to the Los Angeles Police Department on the seat, and put the gun barrel in his mouth and pulled the trigger. Just as he'd seen in the movie, *A Few Good Men*, which President Clinton's friend, Vince Foster (who did it the same way), had also seen.

As it turns out, Eric had had a chance to be in a production of *A Few Good Men* on stage at a theater in Long Beach. But they wanted him to nearly shave his head, as recruits do, and he didn't want to do that nor miss a lot of work at the engineering firm on rehearsals, so he turned it down.

Later when I saw a *60 Minutes* piece on Vince Foster's death and heard his wife talk about him having seen *A Few Good Men,* the producers of the show then proceeded to show a clip of the movie, the scene where the officer commits suicide! I was outraged. *Outraged!*

I could imagine *other* depressed people who were viewing this, watching, and learning, the most effective way for *them* to commit suicide! Completely irresponsible. I considered writing a strong letter protesting the deliberate sensationalism of it, but found I didn't have the energy to take on that particular battle.

Dealing with grief is so emotionally draining and exhausting. It begins to take its toll on you physically. And every other way.

One of Eric's neighbors in the complex had heard the shot and searched the lot until they found him and called the ambulance and the police. Later, his friends in the complex told us what an awful night that had been for all of them as they gathered and watched him being taken away.

By the time we had arrived several days later, Eric's landlord had had the kindness of heart and compassion for us, to have tackled the terrible job of cleaning up Eric's car so we would not have to see any of that when we arrived. I am still so touched by that great act of kindness even now as I write, and it makes me weep grateful tears. Never let anyone tell you that people are not good and kind and caring in this world. They are. They want to help you. Often when they don't even know you.

There were so many complications in trying to straighten out the paperwork on Eric's car (he was still making payments on it), so we finally decided to just turn it back to the loan company and be rid of it. Neither of us could bear being near it anyway, although we did go together to clear out the glove compartment and trunk of the things that were his.

Nightmare after nightmare in the aftermath. Horror after horror.

As it was, we had had to wait anyway until the cremation was performed and we could be given his ashes. I remember the deep, awful dread I felt in having to go back there for that reason. How in the WORLD could I carry my beautiful son around in a brass container? How?

Beforehand, Dick went with me to one of the nice department stores in California, Robinson's-May, to purchase some special picture frames I wanted to give those who had spoken at his funeral, as well as a beautiful, sturdy, black leather case with a handle to put the heavy container in so we could carry it on the airplane inconspicuously, and I could keep him close to me. Oh, the sadness and despair of those awful, awful days.

I remember Dick deciding we needed lunch before returning home with our purchases and with his ashes now inside the new leather bag. I couldn't bear to leave him in the car, so I carried it close to me. It was very, very heavy, just like my heart. The Underwoods, all three of us, have always had a somewhat dry, at times bizarre sense of humor. So it didn't escape either of us that we were, all three, in a manner of speaking "out to lunch" together. No smiles. Just the shared comment and recognition of the fine line between tragedy and comedy, laughter and tears.

I called the airlines ahead of time to ask what to do about carrying the heavy brass container with me onto the airplane . . . and through security. I certainly had no intention of letting him out of my sight or put on some conveyor belt or dark underbelly of an airplane like so much checked luggage. To many I suppose that might seem a bit irrational—after all, it wasn't really Eric there, just his remains. "Cremains"—a new word added grudgingly to my vocabulary. But to me, at the time, it felt like an urgent matter of life and death itself. I carried him close to me, in my lap, the whole long flight back home thinking, with tears streaming, how I would never have dreamed . . . at the time I had carried him inside me with such joy when I was pregnant . . . that one day I would be carrying his remains back home . . .

rested, this time, outside my belly. My heart kept breaking further into pieces every hour of that interminable flight home.

I flashed back in time remembering how happy we had been to find ourselves pregnant. I felt I *knew* exactly when we conceived. We had waited six years until we were ready. Eric and I had gone through a long labor, a long struggle for him to be born, breech. When they handed him to me—at 10:30 in the morning, and I saw his bright blue eyes looking straight at me, I wept for joy. He looked exactly like his daddy! I'd never known such incredible joy.

Our friends, the Bryants and Steadmans, met us at the airport, and, of course, offered immediately to help us carry our bags. They couldn't have known what the black leather bag contained but their well-meaning insistence on taking it from me finally caused me to break away and run on ahead of all of them, crying and clutching the bag to me. I couldn't bear to speak the words to explain to them what was wrong.

The next days at home in South Carolina were filled with calls and visitors and making plans for a second service on September 1, 1995. A memorial for those in our community and the friends he'd grown up with. Again, we had to think of whom to ask to say a few words, arrange for the place, flowers, etc. My sister Janice and her family, her husband David and my niece Lindsey and nephews Ben and Brian drove from Michigan and stayed ahead of time to help us. My mother and stepdad stayed in Michigan to sell their home before moving to Florida. Dick's mother, who was ninety-one and had a broken hip, was unable to make the trip from her home in Plymouth, Michigan. Both of Eric's grandfathers had died years before.

A good friend, Ray, the head of the performing arts department at the university, agreed to preside, and Mark and Hallman, our closest friends, made some wonderful, emotional remarks—recollections of having known Eric since he was a two-year-old.

Dick is a noted Shakespeare scholar and author, so it was natural of him to call up favorite passages. I still don't know how he managed to do it, but he began the service, with Ray at his side, interacting with him:

Dick— *"In one of the greatest metaphors of death, Hamlet calls it 'the undiscovered country from whose bourne no traveler returns.' The words come from a long and complicated soliloquy, but it begins with some lines that show how strongly Hamlet is attached to suicide as a release . . . ."*

Ray— *"To die, to sleep no more and by a sleep to say we end the heartache and the thousand natural shocks that flesh is heir to."*

Dick— *"That's not a natural state of mind, but it was apparently Eric's. The torment of Hamlet happens not to die by his own hand, but still, the best words are those of his friend, Horatio . . . ."*

Ray— *"Good night, sweet prince and flights of angels sing thee to thy rest."*

Dick— *"The other day, driving around on a beautiful, sunny day, I was reminded of how much Eric loved California, and I thought of the last verses of a poem by Wallace Stevens, and it happens to be about a soldier who was killed in World War I, but it's about the cliché, 'life goes on.' Stevens speaks of the young man's death as a time . . ."*

Ray— *" . . . when the wind stops and over the heavens the clouds go nevertheless in their direction."*

Dick— *"The hills east of Burbank were clear and beautiful. My son had cut himself off from this day, the sunlight, the clouds. But what I remember is how sweet he smelled when I used to carry him over my shoulder as a one-year-old.*

"Suddenly he was a big kid and he played tight end, outside linebacker, and when he set the county record for the one hundred ten-high hurdles, I realized I had not embraced him for a long time and how tall and muscular he was. I was filming him when he won the upper state high hurdles and tears came to my eyes. He was peaking just right, and I still think he would have won the state

meet if he hadn't come down with strep throat the week before the race in Columbia.

"Then he was a Vanderbilt graduate, then a transportation engineer. Then an actor. He called me in the summer of 1993 after being best man to his friend, Todd, and said, 'Dad, I got that part in the movie Forrest Gump,' *and I was so happy for him."*

Ray— *"Fear no more the heat of the sun or the furious winter's rages. Thou thy worldly task hast done. Home are gone and taken thy wages. Golden lads and girls all must as chimney sweepers come to dust."*

Several people asked Dick later how he had managed to do that, get up and speak to the crowd, and he said, *"I just knew he would have done it for me."*

Ray went on to say:

"Today we gather to remember and to celebrate the life of a beloved son and friend. If you knew Eric or if you knew about Eric, then you know that he was an exceptional young man. An honors graduate of D.W. Daniel High School as well as Vanderbilt University where he was a double major in civil engineering and math, Eric excelled at virtually everything he attempted. His energy and abilities appeared to know no bounds. He was extremely successful in his career as a transportation engineer, commuting a total of three hours daily in California traffic to his place of work and back, and recently received a rare yet well-deserved mid-year promotion. In the evenings, he pursued his other love—acting— and had indeed made some inroads and progress in that extremely demanding and competitive profession. At the time of his death, he was performing in a showcase in Los Angeles. A quiet and unassuming person, Eric was loved and respected by those whose lives crossed paths with his. His colleagues and friends remember him as talented, compassionate, dedicated, and committed, with a delicious, and at times a bit irreverent, sense of humor not unlike his dad's.

"I know it is extremely difficult if not impossible to understand the tragedy of Eric's death. And while I feel a terribly deep sense of

grief and regret, in particular for Sandy and Dick, I am at a loss as to how to express this. We must inevitably accept the reality of this event as we cannot revisit it and change it. But it is virtually impossible to articulate its tremendous impact on us or to be able to explain it. Thus, all I can do is to leave you with some thoughts and expressions which I collected from my journey in an attempt to try and find some meaning for it.

"I cannot lay this at the feet of an unjust God, for I believe that it is the result of the fallible and imperfect nature we all share as human beings. And if we believe that God is ultimately good and loving and forgiving, as I think we must, then we can rest assured that Eric is just fine, no matter why or how he left this temporal existence. Thus, we come together today to collectively reaffirm the validity and the joy of Eric's life with us. And, as members of the same family, all of whom have our own individual weaknesses, we also gather to collectively share in the responsibility for his loss. Where it touches one of us, it touches all of us.

"So what, then, are we left with? With what do we fill the void? We are left with a renewed respect and appreciation for the sanctity of life and a resolve to do our utmost to preserve it. William Shakespeare has written, 'Love comforteth as sunshine after rain.' And we must reach out in love and support to those who remain, particularly Dick and Sandy. But even more than that, I believe we must be more sensitive, more attentive, and more responsive to the needs of those around us. By doing so, I believe we can be assured that this tragedy can be brought to some sort of meaningful closure that will yet live on in a positive way.

"As a parent, I find a loss such as this particularly difficult to contemplate or try to make sense of. I have recently seen my own children off to their respective colleges, and the other day I walked through their empty rooms just to look around and to think about them. In each room I noticed various memorabilia and pictures which were reminders of events and moments that were important in their lives—things like Sandy and Dick have placed on some of the tables at the back of this hall. And this experience again reaffirmed in me that we are here today not just to mourn Eric's *passing but to remember and to celebrate his short yet vital life. For all who knew Eric and for all whose lives he touched, he will indeed live in our memories forever."*

In addition, Eric's best friend Shane, his college roommate at Vanderbilt, gave a long and wonderful tribute Eric would have loved; and his good friend since grade school, Andy, spoke and shared some great memories as well.

We ran a video of some of the remarks that had been made at the service in California and at the end of the service handed out a two-page information sheet explaining to people (who we knew would be curious) what had happened and what little we knew about it, as well as resources for others they might know who were depressed. We also invited people to visit the tables at the back of the room where we displayed some of Eric's memorabilia and photographs on tall boards that depicted his life from infancy through adulthood.

Before the services, as I went through our photo albums culling pictures to put on the boards, my sister kept checking on me, worried that what I was doing was far too difficult and emotional, bringing back all those memories. And, it was, certainly. But I had a fierce determination for all these people to see that Eric had had a good and happy life and many wonderful experiences . . . and not be remembering him in terms of depression, suicide, and sadness. I would do whatever it took to circumvent that. Again, as before, it was as if I were on an automatic pilot of some sort.

Over the next days and weeks people were wonderful in sending letters and cards of condolences as well as checks and donations for our suicide prevention fund. We sent half the money to the group in Los Angeles I had talked to before leaving there and later received a kind letter of appreciation from the director assuring us they would put the funds to good use in Eric's memory.

Dick and I had both returned to work by now and soon a planning committee was formed—of friends and colleagues—to determine how to use the remainder of the fund for best use in our local community. After several good ideas were put forth, we decided the greatest need was to educate people about depression and suicide and to bring them together to discuss the issues. Part of the fund was used for the luncheon, as well as for the video tapes shown, and to pay for the keynote speaker's honoraria and travel expenses. The planning began in October 1995 and continued through the spring until it was held (in the same hotel ballroom where we had held his September 1995 community memorial service) in August 1996.

CHAPTER EIGHT

At the second service, in Clemson, the life of that happy child and young adult was remembered in the colorful photographs posted on those boards for all to see:

As an infant sleeping sweetly in his crib. Being loved and held and carried around by each of his grandfathers on different occasions. Playing in the water at the lake. Fishing in the upper peninsula of Michigan and holding up a fish he'd caught that was bigger than he was.

Standing, surrounded by huge orange pumpkins one brisk autumn day when he was about three. With his little friends in costumes, trick or treating one Halloween. Playing piano while sitting on daddy's lap. Making a snowman with his little friend next door, Lisa, when they were about three.

A picture with all his smiling classmates at his pre-school. The first day of kindergarten with his little friend, Mike. Summer trips to the ocean every year. Playing in the sand.

Soccer teammates arm in arm. Camping out. Up in the tree house. Sleeping out in the tent in the backyard. Boat rides.

Visits to and from his grandparents'. Piano recitals and awards. Riding his bicycle. Singing in the school choir. Building . . . and flying . . . the model airplanes he had built.

Running high hurdles and winning championships. Playing football. With his homecoming date, with him in his uniform.

His part-Pomeranian, part-poodle puppy, Cocoa. His

girlfriend, Rene, at our house . . . and later, all dressed up for the prom with Rene and with his friend Todd and his date.

High school graduation with his big circle of close friends all smiling together in their caps and gowns. Rene with him and a *"You're Number One"* balloon when he won the upper state track meet. Leaving with his date, Susan, for a dance and dinner date.

Our trip out west following his high school graduation. Standing with his muscular back and broad shoulders to the camera, taking in the awe of Yosemite. Standing, smiling with me, with the Golden Gate Bridge in the background. Our helicopter ride over San Francisco, a thrill for all of us.

Several of his close childhood friends gathered in front of the "Dragon Wagon" (our old station wagon) before taking off for a beach trip following graduation. Eric with his pride and joy, his sports car, a 280Z.

At Vanderbilt with his friend and roommate, Shane. Back at our house on spring break, going to a Rolling Stones concert held here. Graduation at Vanderbilt with Shane and his girlfriend (and later his wife), Jewel.

His first Los Angeles studio apartment. Taking his dad and me out to a movie theater in Los Angeles, standing near the big posters of Tom Hanks and others. Eric and Kay, who he had lived with for a year in another apartment of their own, and with whom he had come close to marrying. With his dad in San Francisco on Pier 49, watching the seals. A drive down the Pacific Coast Highway 1, the scenic seventeen-mile drive . . . standing near the famous lone pine.

Standing with his close friend and co-worker, Ali, at the engineering firm. At a Christmas luncheon with his boss and all his co-worker friends. Our trip together to Catalina Island for a long weekend to visit a comedy club where his friend and caretaker of his apartment complex had a stand-up comedy routine . . . where Dick played the piano.

Our whole family (except for Dick's mom) at North Myrtle

Beach the summer before he died. Him standing near a big poster for the movie *Forrest Gump,* which he'd had a speaking part in.

Looking at those photographs, it seemed as if Eric led a charmed life—tall, smiling, handsome, smart, multi-talented, well-loved by family and friends—successful in nearly everything he undertook. How? How then could any of this ever make any sense? How could he be gone forever?

As soon as we were back in Clemson in late August 1995, people would ask me if I'd seen an episode of *The Oprah Show* that tackled depression and suicide. The episode happened to run soon after Eric died. We had not seen it, of course. We had been in Los Angeles tending to all the gruesome business I have already spoken of here. But a friend of mine managed to get a tape of it for us, and it spoke directly to this issue of how someone so successful, who seemed to have it all, could even *want* to do such a thing.

Again, the issue of suicide had nothing to do with external matters like success or any of the outward trappings of life. It had only to do with the excruciating emotional pain from which there seemed to be no other way to escape.

All of Oprah's guests were highly successful—overachievers all of them. They also had had family and friends who loved and cared about them. Each described how none of that mattered—at all—when their depression took hold.

Each described how their depression became unending despair and hopelessness, creating such pain and darkness that they could hardly bear it. Each described several attempts at suicide, a few as cries for help and attention, but most with the real intent to end it then and there. They were found in time (obviously) and since had worked in various ways to combat their depression. All the stories had a common thread—the overwhelming need to escape the crushing pain.

One man, who had, coincidentally, been a winning coach at Clemson at one time, made a serious attempt on his life on his young daughter's birthday. Oprah seemed shocked and asked *how* he could do such a thing knowing it would cause her so much pain for the rest of her life—on her birthday? The answer was—as most who make such attempts say—his depression and pain didn't allow him any room or opening to think about anything else but how to get the pain to stop. He would never have wanted to hurt her in that way, but neither was he able to think about such things as what day it was and how it would affect everyone else. This is corroborated, case after case, in various studies.

Seeing that tape—like all the other information that was coming my way—helped us a great deal as we struggled to understand the insidiousness of suicide's primary cause—depression.

Not knowing how else to help me, my sister, Janice, launched a massive research effort of her own on depression and suicide and sent me all kinds of articles and books and reading materials. It was very touching, and she said it helped her as well. Eventually, I was to learn from her—later on—that she had long suffered from the same such deep depressions and had been close to suicide herself at times.

We realized that our father had most likely, looking back, suffered from depression. He had died young, at age fifty-seven, from many years of heart disease. One of his sisters had been hospitalized at one time with her own depression. And my husband's cousin had attempted suicide and was a depressive all her life; another cousin completed his suicide.

So Eric had this lethal predisposition for depression from both sides of the family—and we were never even aware of it. Medical science now believes depression and suicide are caused by complex factors having to do with genetic predisposition coupled with environmental/cultural causes. The difficulty with depression and suicide is that each person and situation is so uniquely individual—both in causes and degree, and in the ability to apply treatments successfully.

One of the most helpful pieces of information I read was

from a woman, Adina Wrobleski, who had also lost a child to suicide. Her extensive research and straightforward writings about her findings greatly appealed to me and stayed with me.

She was the first I read to point out, for example, that people who get cancer, or heart disease, or lung disease, or kidney disease, all have easily identifiable and "acceptable" understandings of what they were fighting. But, just as the lung, the heart, the kidneys, and the liver can become diseased, so, too, can the brain become diseased. It's just that because it is the brain, the consequences are often more complex, more subtle, and more difficult to treat than with other organs.

Wrobleski, Adina. *Suicide: Survivors. A Guide For Those Left Behind.* Minneapolis: Adina Wrobleski, 1994.

CHAPTER NINE

Slowly, slowly, following the second service in September 1995, the cocoon of shock began to fall away leaving us exposed to our harsh new reality. Dick seemed, outwardly anyway, to be doing much better than I was. With medication, his doctor had stabilized his blood pressure. He began walking a half hour each day on the campus.

Meanwhile, my first thought on waking each morning was, *I wish I were dead. I wish I were dead. I wish I were dead.*

I was back to work but walking around as if shell-shocked. Physically, things were not good. I had never had a problem with high blood pressure before. Now it was sky high and didn't seem to respond to medication. Several doctors all said it was, understandably, "grief-related" and would likely settle down in a month or so. Meantime, not really knowing all the symptoms of menopause, I thought the fact that I was bleeding every day was to be expected. It was only later when my closest friend, Jo, said, *"Sandy, that's not normal. You'd better tell your doctor,"* that I decided to go. When I did, I was told the bleeding was as though my whole body was weeping with the loss of my son—my body reacting physically, as well as emotionally, to my grief.

(Unfortunately, it was then that I began taking Prempro, as recommended to me, and I continued taking it for six and a half years, resulting later on in breast cancer and a radical mastectomy.)

In addition, beginning on my fifty-third birthday, December 14, 1995, four months after Eric died, some strange things began happening to me. For the past few years I had treated myself with a plane ticket out to Los Angeles to spend my birthday with Eric and to begin the Christmas holidays a little early. Dick would join us when finals were over and after he'd turned in his students' grades.

How I dreaded this first birthday without Eric, knowing I'd have been off on an airplane, he would have greeted me at the airport and would have taken me back to his apartment where he'd have presents ready for me and a banner and balloons printed with, HAPPY BIRTHDAY, MOM!

By the time of this birthday, I had, for a couple of months now, been suicidal myself. Seriously so. Nothing seemed to relieve the pain. Nothing. Even knowing all too well the effect it would have on my dear husband, Dick, and our families. I, too, could only think of how I could escape this excruciating pain. I couldn't imagine a life on Prozac or other medication. But mostly, as much as I loved my husband, I couldn't imagine a life without my son. No future seemed to emerge. At least not one worth living for.

My dear friends, Jo and Jon Lee, invited me out to a restaurant for dinner to celebrate my birthday, to take my mind off things. I remember thinking, as I interacted with them and worked at not being a wet blanket, that it was clear how much they wanted me to be the same wise-cracking, sociable friend I'd always been in the past. They wanted the best for me. They wanted me to be normal again. I knew that person was gone. I didn't grieve that fact really. I just knew she no longer existed, and I would never be the same again.

When they dropped me off at home that night, I went into

the bathroom and found that Dick had propped up a small package that had come in the mail next to the mirror where I'd be sure to see it. I reached for it and *Zap!* It felt just as though I'd been struck by lightning—I was jolted a few feet back! I was shocked (this was no static electricity I was talking about); it felt like an electric shock must feel. What was *happening?* What had happened? I stood there for a few minutes stunned, and then I finally went and sat down to open it.

The package contained some information from a woman I had met through a professional Internet online networking conference I had originally joined in connection with my work. After Eric died, I found a separate, private conference on the same network whose members were some of these same people, and I began sharing Eric's story and our grief in an item I had started about him and what had happened. I borrowed the idea from a man who had already been there talking about having lost his only child in a car accident more than a year before. People who joined his online discussion had been helping him with his grief, and so I began talking as well. I consider the people who helped me there at that time a vital part of my life and survival.

After hearing me talk there about how talented and accomplished Eric was, the woman who had sent the package had identified Eric as likely a highly gifted young man. She said her research had shown that the incidence of depression and suicide tended to be much higher for these people—people who excel, who are perfectionists, who are highly sensitive and idealistic. People who are vulnerable and who feel they don't know exactly where they fit in in the world.

This woman had an exceptionally gifted son and, in learning how to help him, she had acquired knowledge and became a consultant to parents of other gifted children. Her expertise was highly regarded. She'd published widely on the subject, and she was a popular speaker at noted programs and conferences throughout the United States.

Later when I asked, she immediately agreed to be the keynote speaker for our community conference on depression the following year. What she was sharing with me now in the package were some of her own writings outlining her spiritual beliefs as well as the journey she'd been on. As I read, I felt amazed to find so many similarities to my own. Incredible. Her exploration of the new sciences beginning with quantum physics. Her moving away from and beyond organized religion and exploring Eastern thought and other religions and beliefs. To my surprise, they all mirrored my own, almost exactly. What (if anything) did this mean? In addition, she had told us she had been a depressive all of her life and had come close to suicide herself more than once. She understood. She wanted to help.

One night when Dick was gone to a meeting, I found I was beginning to panic and felt lost and suicidal, so I called her on the phone for the first time even though we'd never met in person. She knew exactly what to say and managed to calm me down, and told me to breathe. To relax and take deep breaths. To breathe. She kept talking, making perfect sense in the things she said and, with her understanding, that crisis passed. I felt I'd found a friend. Someone who understood like no one else had seemed to. I was extremely grateful and relieved of the tremendous stress of all that was going on all at once.

In the meantime, strange things had continued to happen to me ever since that lightning jolt on my birthday. When we returned home from Los Angeles both Dick and I had become restless sleepers and were up and down, up and down all night long, often at different times, disturbing each other. So I had moved into Eric's room to sleep. And to read. And sometimes, to write.

The thought processes of the parents of a child who has completed suicide are torturous, as I have said. Anything and everything goes through your head. And becomes a worry. (Or an accusation.) What if I'd done this? If I had done that, would that have prevented this? What about that time when . . . ? On and on. Never ending. I have come to believe this is not only an inevitable part of the grief process, it is also a necessary one. To explore every crevice of one's mind and heart to search out the possibility of having caused or contributed to this tragic outcome. Unpleasant, unfriendly territory. One that must be visited and passed through nevertheless. A whole new painful reality to be faced head on. Facing the abyss.

What I would find happening to me in that bed at night bespoke madness to me. I was losing my mind! I was convinced of that. At times I would be awakened out of a sound sleep with my whole body beginning to shake, and I'd feel jolts of energy moving down and through my body and out my feet. Powerful! There were times I even had spontaneous orgasms (absolutely without ever having touched myself). I'd begin crying, along with the shaking, and then I'd laugh out loud and then I'd have to write—whole poems would come out, nearly finished pieces! I was truly terrified that I was losing my mind. This even happened at work at times. Once I was sitting calmly and quietly at my desk in my office looking at the computer screen, my (conscious) mind on work, when zap!—more shaking, and once even another orgasm . . . in broad daylight!—completely out of the blue! What was happening to me? Was I being punished? Was I going mad? Was I possessed?

One night when I awoke and this began happening, and I was shaking and out of control, I thought maybe if I started reading, my mind could divert its attention away from it and alter or stop the physical effects. I was feeling quite terrified when I reached for a book (I've been a voracious reader all my life so my nightstand and the floor by the bed are always stacked with books).

To my astonishment, when I opened the book—by Stan Grof called *The Holotropic Mind* explaining human consciousness—there, in the place where I had stopped reading it, probably a year before, was Eric's face staring back at me! It was a clipping from the local paper with his picture announcing his appearance in the movie *Forrest Gump*. As I started to read the chapter marked by his picture, I found that the page that followed described *kundalini*, an experience of spiritual opening and energy that could, on some occasions—such as the shocking death of one's only child—occur spontaneously.

Known mostly in the East by those practicing yoga and those whose spiritual practice required great discipline and daily practice, here was a description of exactly what had been happening to me—pointed out to me . . . by my son! It was as if he wanted to reassure me that I was *not* crazy. He wanted me to know *why* I was zapped by lightning on my birthday upon reading about a spiritual path similar to my own. He wanted me to know there is so much more going on than this immediate material reality and dimension alone. He wanted me to open up my mind and to expand my consciousness and awareness. At the end of the book, in fact, was a whole chapter by another noted scientist, Itzhak Bentov, who was the first to research, study, and document *kundalini* experiences in the West.

I believe Eric especially wanted me to know, in this way, that he is all right. He wanted me to know it WAS him I had heard in his apartment as I lay on his couch that first night in Los Angeles, *"You best Mama. You best Mama,"* his term of endearment for me when he was alive. I was NOT simply imagining things. I was truly stunned by this amazing synchronicity—one of many, many more I was to experience in the months and years to follow, each a signal from the loving universe and from Eric, "You're on the right track. Keep going."

The woman I had called before when I was in trouble and upset, the one who was to be our keynote speaker at the conference, the expert on gifted children, had mentioned that she would refer me to a therapist friend of hers who also had had some psychic powers since childhood and who might be able to help me with some of these strange, unsettling symptoms by telephone from another state. By then I had also started to see a psychotherapist in a nearby town to work through my grief, but because she had formerly been a nun, I was reluctant to go into the strangeness of what was happening to me with her, believing as I did that her thinking would be more conventional and not so open to believing such wild occurrences.

Again, to mirror Eric's own dilemma, it is hard to expose oneself to the possibility of hearing someone thinking you're *"crazy."* I actually *felt* crazy. I actually believed I was losing my mind. I felt I was being swallowed up by grief and despair.

In addition to the crushing grief and sense of loss, survivors of suicide are left with experiencing others' awkwardness in knowing how (or not) to interact with you. Some people say nothing and go the other way if they see you coming (and sometimes you're grateful not to have to talk to them and yet feel hurt by it at the same time). Some want *too* much to talk and drag out of you all the "juicy," sensational details. Some say exactly the wrong things.

And still others react perfectly—with an "I'm thinking of you" or a gentle touch on the arm and a smile not wanting to pry, just trying to comfort and let you know they're there. The whole situation is simply exasperatingly impossible for everyone. In the end, the people who help the most are those who, without much fanfare, let you know they care, are sorry for your loss, and will be there if you need them.

Often we would hear, *"I can't imagine what you're going through. They say the loss of a child is the worst loss of all. I'm so so sorry for what you're going through."* It was a very lonely time. Instinctively, I knew some sort of group support from other survivors might help, but I dreaded the idea of talking about it face-to-face with strangers.

Finally, at work one day, I called a listing for a survivors' group an hour's drive away. The man who answered sounded nice enough but (as we are in the Bible belt with a large population of Southern Baptists) spoke a good deal in religious terms which, at that time, I was in no mood to hear.

Later, I finally did go to one of these groups, only to confirm my suspicions when they began talking about their worries that their loved ones were *"burning in hell"* as they believed the Bible told them suicides would. That was it for me. No, thank you. There was enough ignorance in the world already about depression and what causes people—sick people—to go through with suicide. I didn't have the emotional stamina to try to set them straight or enlighten them enough to achieve tolerance and understanding. They were hurting, too, obviously, but I had no patience for such nonsense.

In fact, as I sat there in my office before making that first call, I found myself feeling really angry. How had my life come to this? All this grief, sadness, guilt, pain, and loss. Is this what life was to be from now on? My new label *"survivor"* felt less a proud statement of what one could withstand and go on than it did to label a rather sad, pathetic, victim-type. The very idea of that made me furious. I would *not* have it! I was totally resistant to the new reality that was my life now.

As I've said, I never did say, why me? Why us? Why did this happen to us? It seemed all too obvious: why not? Why *not* you? Why should *your* lives be spared of the pain and sorrow other people know?

Yet at the same time, I realized I'd have to be dragged kicking and screaming before making any effort to join the ranks of those whose lives now seemed to be defined by their loved one's suicide. The whole thing seemed impossible enough to live with, without choosing to allow oneself to be sucked into some awful vortex of pain and become lost forever in the same kind of darkness. It was becoming quite clear to me that learning how to live with all of this would take a lot of work. A whole lot.

CHAPTER TEN

The truth is, despite several tries that proved unsatisfactory—or unsuited to me at least—help was there for us, in many forms. The group, of approximately thirty or so people from all around the country on the Internet conference kept me going. All strangers. Remarkable, really. I'd never laid eyes on any of them. Well, except one, a co-founder of the group, whom I'd met at one of the World Future Society Conferences I had participated in, in connection with my strategic planning work at the university.

I was developing some friendships and bonds with several of them who never seemed to fail me. Always there when I needed them. Sometimes I'd drive down to the office in the middle of the night just to connect with them as they helped me through it with great patience and compassion.

I honestly believe that some of these people saved my life. They got me past my own ideation of suicide, my plans for how I'd do it. I could, for example, see a beam high above my desk, and I knew I could throw a rope over it and kick the chair away and be done with it. Then it wouldn't be Dick who found me and our home wouldn't be tainted with it, but, I thought, maybe the janitors would find me early the next morning. And then I did worry it might be one of the dear young women who reported to me for ten years now and who were like my daughters. How could I do that to them? Too awful in the imagining.

believe that meeting her and the friendship we have now is the real reason I was led to that conference.)

Sitting there, hearing all those stories, I was shocked! I couldn't *believe* what I was hearing and the suffering it represented. Some horrible, awful stories, of even very young children. So much pain. So much enveloping, overwhelming pain. I had had no idea there was so much pain in the world. I seemed to be taking it all in at once. I felt completely undone. I sobbed all the way to the elevator and all the way back up to our room.

I realized for the first time how little I really knew about life. I had lived for fifty-three years obliviously happy and self-satisfied. After all, I had everything. Besides my wonderful, talented husband and son, I had a job I loved and a career to be proud of that I had created and which allowed me to travel all over the country. Good, close friends. Our family in Michigan and Florida. A nice place to live. A comfortable future. A safe, happy little cocoon. Now exploded to smithereens!

I knew little of sickness and pain and trouble and worry. I certainly didn't give much thought to death. Dick and I had both lost our fathers, mine at fifty-seven in 1977 and Dick's at seventy-six in 1980. And those were, to be sure, terrible losses and very painful at the time. But they fell into the natural order of things. One expects to lose one's grandparents and parents eventually. One does not expect, or prepare for, losing one's child—which is *not* in the *"natural order of things."* Although, of course, it was. And happens all the time to lots of people. I'd just never been exposed to it firsthand.

Part of the emotional and physical roller coaster *is* having one's whole world turned upside down and one's whole reality destroyed forever. How to rebuild? How to gain one's footing even? How to *survive* this nuclear devastation? It feels overwhelming because it really *is*. And only now, years later, can I see that it was a necessary jolt, a necessary rebuilding. A necessary introduction to a whole new reality and a whole new understanding of what life is and requires of us.

Chance, Sue, M.D. *Stronger Than Death. When Suicide Touches Your Life: A Mother's Story.* New York: W.W. Norton & Co., 1992.

Since our small town is located on large Lake Hartwell, I decided it'd be best if I drove my car to the public beach nearby and walk out into the water, swim out too far, and drown myself. That was "the plan" I'd devised and kept hidden from everyone when Dick and I drove to Atlanta—just as we had done earlier, unawares, on the day Eric died—to our doctor there for a checkup since we were both feeling like physical as well as mental wrecks since Eric died.

The whole two-hour drive there, I was filled with thoughts of suicide. The pain was just too excruciating to go on living with it.

Dr. W. was a kindly, older physician whom we didn't know well since we'd only been seeing him on the recommendation of one of Dick's friends a couple of years before.

We each were put in separate examining rooms, and Dr. W. saw Dick first and had learned from him what had happened before he came in my room to see me.

He entered the room saying how sorry he was, and I burst into tears. He immediately came over to me, with tears in his eyes and put his arms around me to comfort me. He told me his brother had completed suicide years before, and, as a physician, he had thought at the time that he had to be the one in control and had managed to get through the funeral and help his family members. But the truth was, he said, he knew he had never really faced up to it and dealt with its effect on him. He'd buried it and he knew now that had been a mistake.

The whole drive home, I felt like a new woman. I couldn't believe it. This man, with his understanding and by saying just the right words, had saved my life! I felt he had, quite literally, saved my life! Like an angel, he was there with exactly the right words just as I was sinking to my lowest point.

Time and again over the next months, this would occur—I'd sink again to some new low point only to be rescued or buoyed up by someone out there ready to catch me from a fatal fall.

I was on an emotional roller coaster ride most of the time in those first months after Eric died. When I got back to work, for example, one of the things that began happening was, I knew, of my own making, yet I seemed to be unable to stop it. Eric took his life on a Thursday evening at around 5:30 P.M. One Thursday, early on, I began re-enacting that afternoon in my mind, imagining him talking to his boss, leaving work early, driving to the gun store to pick up the gun, going home and putting on his workout clothes, putting the gun in his bag, taking the letters to the mail slots in the apartment, waving hello to his landlady, and going out to his car. I imagined him sitting there in his car, looking at that little tree, taking out the gun . . . .

Over and over these scenes played themselves out in my head. It was like watching a horror movie and not being able to stop what was going on before my eyes . . . not being able to look away. I began to dread Thursdays. The *"howling hounds of Thursdays"* I called it. They would come after me. To torture me. A living nightmare. This went on for weeks and weeks.

Intellectually, I understood it was my mind creating this— what? To try somehow to stop him from going through with it? To take back control? I didn't know. I just knew that I was unable to get it to stop, and I was becoming paralyzed and terrorized by it, knowing that as the week dragged on, eventually Thursday would be there again, and I would have to live through my son's suicide all over again.

The therapist (and others after her) told me it was post-traumatic stress disorder due to the grief and that, eventually, it would go away. Small comfort during those awful, miserable weeks.

Then, one Thursday I was on-line with the conference group I've mentioned, and one of those who were following my item posted a touching poem he had written for us. Other people began commenting on it, and I did as well, and I glanced over at the clock and saw that "the time" had come and gone, and I had been free of the "visions" and images I'd been having! I had been so engrossed in what everyone was talking about and his kindness to us that this time, on this Thursday, I hadn't fallen back into my "horror movie" re-enacting what Eric had gone through on that awful Thursday in August. And, the following Thursday . . .

and those thereafter . . . I no longer had to go through that an more. I'd been "saved" from that horror which now had passe thanks to his . . . to all their . . . kindnesses to me. It felt like strange, wonderful, freeing sort of miracle.

Clearly, clearly the universe was helping me and was the loving benevolent caretaker I always used to believe it was. Slowly my faith was being rebuilt and strengthened as occurrence afte occurrence, experience after experience, synchronicity afte synchronicity kept happening.

As we continued at work to meet and plan the community conference on depression, one of my friends, a colleague who was helping me gave me a book by a woman, Sue Chance, who lived in our area. Sue Chance was a medical doctor whose son, also an only child, had killed himself. I called and talked with her and she recommended we consider going to the national meeting of survivors of suicide that year, 1995, which was being held in November in Richmond, Virginia. She said with our backgrounds at the university we could most likely benefit from the first day's discussion by the University of Virginia doctors and others who could give us information and statistics on depression and suicide. She also felt we'd meet other people in our situation who we could talk to and who could help.

Looking back, immediately after we attended at least, I had felt it was mostly a mistake having attended. It had been only three months since Eric died and the whole experience of the conference was so overwhelming and so extremely emotional. There was one evening meeting, for example (from which Dick had begged off) that I went to alone. It was a gathering of all the parents of children who had completed suicide. As we sat in a large circle and went around the room and tearfully told our stories, we heard some thirty or forty different stories, all of them heart-wrenching.

(Later on I became lifelong friends with Pat, one of the women I met there that night who had also lost her son and who later sought me out to give me comfort and help me. I now

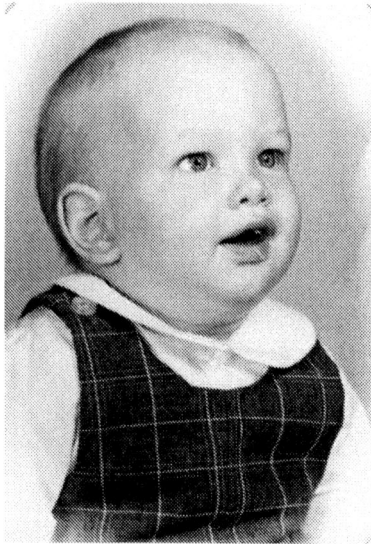

Eric's baby picture, 1969

The Underwoods—Dick, Eric, and Sandy when Eric was a baby.

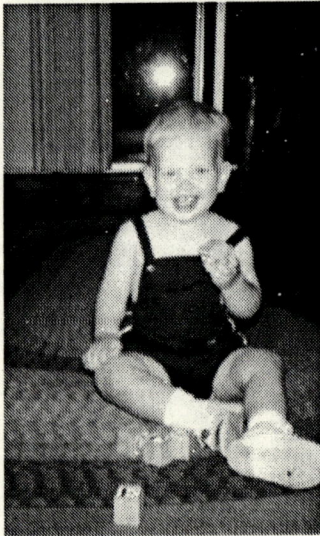

Eric, grinning baby, with building blocks, in our apartment in married housing, Ann Arbor, Michigan where he was born

Building with his blocks

With Daddy, playing the piano

Picking out a pumpkin for Halloween

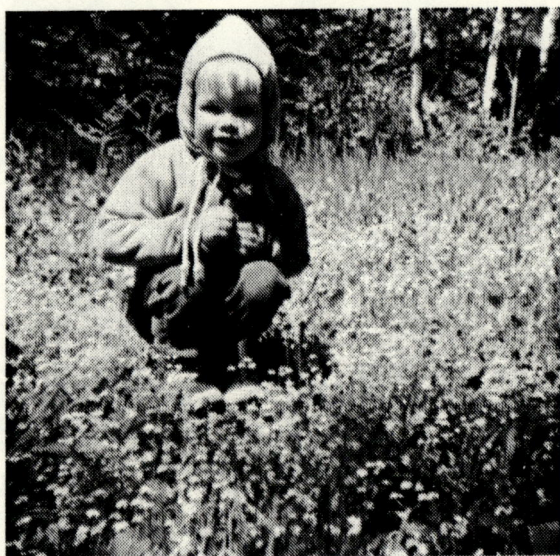

Eric in a field of forget-me-nots in the U.P. of Michigan

At the ocean in North Myrtle Beach where we spent our summers

Caught a fish at Murphy Lake, where Grandma and Grandpa Underwood had a summer cabin in the U.P. of Michigan

More fishing at Murphy Lake, this time a big one

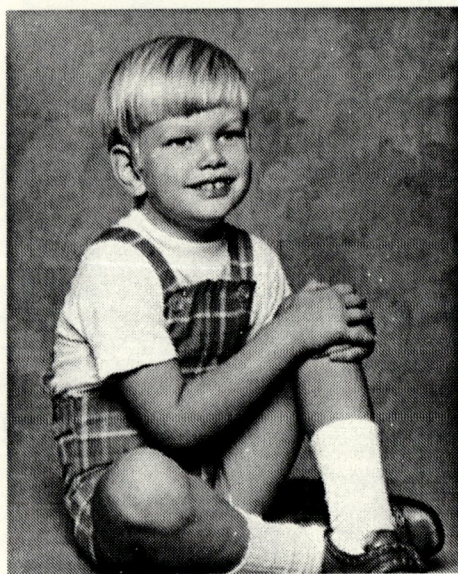

Eric at around age five

In his Sunday suit, Eric at around age six

The Underwoods—Dick, Eric, and Sandy when Eric was around age thirteen

Flying one of the model radio-controlled airplanes
Eric built, here with his friend, Todd

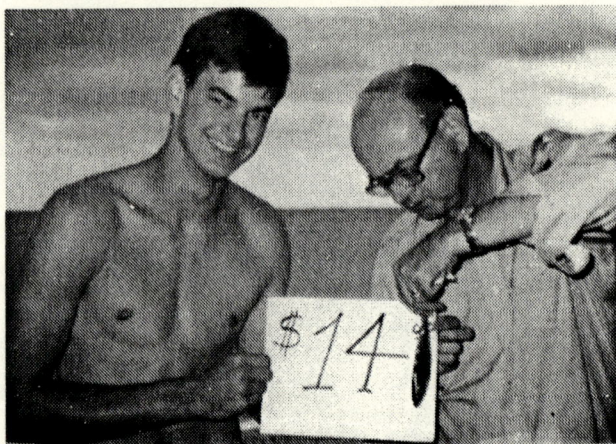

Dad and Eric at the ocean. The $14 sign represents what
Dick had estimated the fish cost after buying licenses, bait,
going out in the boat, etc.

With his young cousins, Ben and Brian, at the ocean one
summer when Eric was a teenager

Reading to his little cousins, Lindsey and Ben, before leaving
for a family trip to the ocean

Eric on the back porch of the home we moved to a year after
he died. With his friends celebrating Jean Lee's birthday
when they were around fifteen.

The high hurdles upper state track meet.
Eric won first place and set a record, 1986.

Celebrating the record with his dad, 1986

After they won their football game and the conference championship (the first undefeated regular season in Daniel High's history), 1985

Senior prom night out by the flowering dogwoods with his lovely date, Rene

Eric with his devoted Samoyed dog, Sasha

Eric graduates from Vanderbilt University with honors and a double major in engineering and math, 1990

Seeing California for the first time on our trip there following graduation, 1986. Eric with me at the Golden Gate Bridge in San Francisco.

Eric discovering the wonders of Yosemite, 1986

Eric at the lone pine, on the Pacific Coast Highway 1, in 1991

ERIC MICHAEL UNDERWOOD

One of the photographs Eric used during his acting career
to send to casting directors, agents, and others, 1994

Upper Panther Meadow, Mount Shasta, California where
the ceremony was held and I scattered his ashes to return
him home to California, 1997

CHAPTER ELEVEN

We buried Dick's ninety-one-year-old mother, in Michigan, six months to the day from the day our only child, our son, had died. In the middle of our grief, here was more grief to deal with. My heart went out to my husband realizing what must be going through his head and heart. His son. Now, his mother. It seemed too much to take on all at once. We had had Eric's furniture and belongings shipped back to our small house. The boxes were stacked wherever we could manage, and now—since Dick was an only child—we had all his parents' big house full of things as well.

I tried to deal with what I could, taking off more time from work for the funeral and to deal with the house in Michigan, but my own growing depression at the time left me feeling totally overwhelmed and exhausted, especially since I was back to work full time now. A close relative suggested we have someone come in and hold an auction to sell everything, but I knew how that would have broken Dick's mother's heart so we decided to just move it all back to South Carolina.

Dick said we'd have to look for another, bigger house back home, and we found one we liked, on the lake, and we moved in in May of 1996. When I first walked down to the dock and looked out at the lake, I burst into tears. There, directly across the lake, was the public beach—the same beach where, several months before, in the early hours of one January morning, I had gotten out of the car in the dark and walked to the shore with the idea of drowning myself to escape my own excruciating pain. Dick had been out of town, in Michigan, and had no idea what had been going on in my mind. I couldn't burden him with that. The pain was so great and the future so hopeless I could see no way to live through it or to go on living with it. As he was to return the next day, I knew he'd find Sasha in time so she'd be taken care of.

However, as before (when I'd found the kindly doctor who held me while I cried and who said exactly the right thing to me), again I was saved by angels. I started sobbing as I recalled all the words of help and encouragement I had been getting from my Internet conference friends and realized I just couldn't do it. I couldn't go through with my plan to just walk out into the water until it was over my head and drown. Instead, I drove to my office and sat at the computer and sobbed, both because it felt like I hadn't had the courage to escape this pain and because, at the same time, I was relieved I hadn't been able to go through with it.

And now here I was, in May 1996, on the opposite side of the lake at our lovely new home, looking over at that same public beach directly across from us, and I was still alive! I had lived through that lowest of my low points.

After having lived in this lake house for more than a year, Eric's friend, Todd, visited and told us that he and Eric had been to parties in this very house when they were kids! They had gone swimming off our dock! And, years later, a woman—who had owned the house for many years and was the mother of one of Eric's friends—sent us a packet of photographs of Eric and her daughter and their friends celebrating her birthday on the back porch. *Our* back porch! The very same house! Although the town *is* small (some 16,000 people), what are the odds of us finding, and buying, a house that our son (unbeknownst to us) had had some happy times in as a teenager? Mere coincidence? I don't think so!

Gradually I came to understand that my own experience of that horrible pain and my own depression and suicidal thoughts were actually, in a sense, a *gift*, as clichéd as that term has become. What *other* way could I have learned or understood how—how—our son could have done such a thing? Now, through my *own* experience, I knew. Now I understood. I was experiencing the depth of pain he had had, the pain that must be escaped. The pain that was impossible to live with. The difference was that my pain and depression were grief-related. Eric's was more complicated with many different contributing factors.

All my adult life—especially after having worked for twenty-five years at a scientific and academic research university—I had looked to science, and now I looked to medical science for answers. Now, as I was beginning to experience a new reality, a new understanding of life (and death), I realized I would have to learn how to accept that there *were* no answers for some of my questions. Some things are beyond knowing at this level of being and may only be known and comprehended at the soul level. Perhaps in another dimension. Perhaps at death. Perhaps where Eric *did* go when he died.

As I've said, so many strange, new things were happening to me, it was becoming next to impossible to ignore where I felt I was being led, what I felt I was being shown . . . the expanded reality and consciousness I had begun to experience. Gradually, some of the pieces were beginning to fit together for me.

For example, beginning in the 1970s, I had been drawn inexplicably to begin reading science magazines and books. My background and interests had been in the liberal arts and in political science. I knew very little of the hard sciences. Yet, here I was, being drawn to read far beyond my level of understanding. Books by Gary Zukav, *The Dancing Wu Li Masters;* by Fritjof Capra, *The Tao of Physics;* William James' *The Varieties of Religious Experience;* Fred Alan Wolf's *Taking the Quantum Leap: The*

New Physics for Non-Scientists; and even the Jane Roberts books about Seth who said, *"You create your own reality."*

All these ideas excited me and pushed me further and further into readings that went beyond and challenged traditional Western science and religious dogma. Learning about the Eastern religions in particular helped address for me the questions I had had as a twelve-year-old being baptized, immersed in water, and told that only those who accept Jesus Christ as their personal savior will get into heaven and know God . . . (everyone else will burn in hell).

Why? I remember thinking silently as a young girl. Why would God create a world with so many people—in Africa and China and all the other places where they didn't know about Jesus—only to let them burn in hell? What kind of God was *that?* Those nagging, legitimate questions kept me searching for answers and the most likely source at the time seemed to me to be science.

What captured my imagination and interest were such things as Niels Bohr's *complementarity* (e.g., a coin has two sides, but just because you can't see them both at the same time, doesn't mean the other side doesn't exist) and Heisenberg's *uncertainty principle*, with the role of the observer affecting outcomes (as Seth said, we create our reality). And, the findings of quantum physics which found that at the very most minute, microscopic levels, nothing is there! . . . Or, that is, that matter can be either a particle or a wave, or both and is ever-changing.

I remember sitting in my favorite chair reading Capra's *Tao of Physics* in about 1980 with tears streaming down my face in recognition that things were beginning to make sense, when my husband walked into the room and commented as I told him how excited I was, yet still mystified as to WHY I kept being drawn to reading all this science. He said I reminded him of that guy in the movie *Close Encounters of the Third Kind* who kept excitedly building a mashed potato mound that looked like the Devil's Tower in Wyoming . . . He knew not why (he had never been there . . . yet); he only knew that he *"had"* to go there. Exactly! I was so touched that Dick understood! He'd made the connection and he "got" how important this was to me. My dear, dear husband who loves me so. I was (and am) so lucky to have him.

Through the years, I was eventually able to meet several of these scientists, usually as guest speakers at one of my professional conferences, or later, at one of the healing conferences: Fritjof Capra, Rupert Sheldrake, Stanislav Grof, Hank Wesselman, Deepak Chopra, Gary Zukav, Brian Arthur, and others.

And, though I haven't met him in person, I did spend more than an hour and a half speaking on the telephone to another of my favorites, Fred Alan Wolf, a physicist whose books I've been reading since the 1980s. I had sent him an e-mail about something he had written about suicide and told him I would be in San Francisco for a meeting in 1997, and he encouraged me to call him so we could discuss it. He was most gracious, and though I was conscious of taking up his time, he was unhurried and very kind to me. He had also lost a son. By the time we finished talking, he had asked me to consider him as my friend now. And he commented on *"the rich fabric of your life since your son died,"* which I thought was a lovely way to put it and which meant so much to me. I felt moved and inspired by our conversation and by his kindness toward me.

And, it was in the early 1990s that this continuing exploration of science and my reading about the new sciences led me to read even more widely and become fascinated in particular with chaos theory and complexity.

At about the same time, in 1990, that our son graduated from Vanderbilt and was heading off to California for his first job, I was being introduced to chaos theory, which is often described using the metaphor of a butterfly's wings fluttering which, in turn, could ultimately cause a hurricane to occur as far away as Tokyo (this is also known as *"the butterfly effect"*). The point is that we are all intimately connected and what each of us does has more far-reaching effects than we could ever imagine.

It was, in fact, through the Chaos (Internet) Conference—which I first learned of at the World Future Society Conference in 1992—that eventually led me to the group mentioned earlier who helped me through my grief when Eric died.

I came to look back on all of that earlier exploration into science as having been a sort of sub-conscious preparation for me to better understand and prepare me for what was to come (Eric's suicide).

It was, in fact, the very special knowledge of chaos theory that ultimately helped me to understand the ambiguity in realizing that our ingrained habits of thinking in terms of either/or is wrong-headed—at the most profound level. I believe it isn't an issue of EITHER/OR—that is, predestination/fate versus (or) free will—it is BOTH/AND. A shocking *"truth"* that came to me after seeing the movie Eric was in, *Forrest Gump*. At the end of the movie, Forrest stands at Jenny's grave and says to her (in effect): *"I see now, Jenny, Captain Dan said it was his destiny to die in war, yet Mama always told me that no matter what, I could do anything I put my mind to. But I don't know. I think they both are right."*

I have learned over many years of experience now that there *are* no coincidences in this life. No *"accidents."* It was no mere coincidence that my son had had a role in this movie a year before he died and that that truth was part of it. It was no mere coincidence that I had been studying just such ideas *before* Eric died. All those years were in preparation for the life lessons and experiences I have come here to earth to learn from. The most important ones were the most painful ones. And, I could never have learned or come to accept them any other way.

102

CHAPTER TWELVE

The community conference on depression we put together with the funds our friends had collected or given, was held nearly a year to the day from when Eric died, in August 1996. It was a great success.

What had started out to be targeted for a small audience grew to more than 200 participants. In fact, we had requests from nearly 400, but the ballroom we had reserved would seat no more than 200 at tables. The response to the program and the need it represented was very gratifying for every one who had worked so hard on it. The event was even covered by some local papers.

— The Messenger

Commentary

Couple turns son's tragedy into way to help other youth

Eric Michael Underwood would have been 28 years old today.

Underwood, who graduated from Daniel High School in 1986, was born on June 3, 1968. This morning, his spirit quietly rests in Pickens County.

Eric, the son of Richard and Sandra Underwood, both employees of Clemson University, died a year ago because of a self-inflicted gunshot. Richard is a Clemson University professor, while Sandra is director of strategic planning at the university.

DAN BRANNAN

EDITOR

same time doing some part-time acting in Hollywood. Eric had always been successful, graduating with honors from Daniel High

went into shock, not believing what they had heard.

Eric had been depressed about a relationship at the time of the shooting. Sandra says Eric did the acting of his life, hiding how depressed he actually was inside.

Last November, Sandra came in touch with nationally known author Stephanie S. Tolan after Eric's death.

Tolan is the co-author of *"Guiding the Gifted Child,"* which has sold 90,000 copies.

Tolan helped Sandra understand how her son could be suffering through

Eric was in Los Angeles at the time of the shooting, working as an engineer and actor. Eric was Richard and Sandra's only child.

Eric's mother told me her son had suffered from depression bouts three or four times since his senior year in college at Vanderbilt University.

Eric was a gifted individual, to say the least. Those familiar with the movie, "Forrest Gump," will remember Eric for his role as the mail call sergeant.

Forrest Gump role

Eric's character brought mail to Forrest, played by Tom Hanks, and Lieutenant Dan. Forrest was busy eating an ice cream cone when Eric handed him his mail, mostly undelivered letters from his love, Jenny.

Sandra said she and her husband were thrilled when their son was in the movie. Unbelievably, Eric was working full-time in his engineering career and at the School and Vanderbilt University; playing on an Upperstate championship football team and capturing the Upperstate 110-meter high hurdle championship in high school.

Eric and his parents were very close. Eric talked to his parents several times a week and his parents did not detect how seriously depressed he actually had become.

During his last bout with depression, Eric had purchased a handgun. In California there is a 15-day waiting period. On the 15th day, Eric shot himself.

Unforgettable knock

The Underwoods will never forget waking up a year ago at 1:30 in the morning to a Clemson police officer at their front door.

The officer told them they needed to contact the Los Angeles police and that their son had shot himself and was dead.

Both Richard and Sandra depression. Sandra credits Tolan with saving her life after Eric's shooting.

The Underwoods wanted to do something in Eric's memory to help others avoid the terrible tragedy they had incurred.

The couple established a memorial for Eric and decided to split the funds between assisting a suicide prevention cause in Los Angeles and presenting a seminar primarily for educators Tuesday at Clemson House Hotel.

The Underwoods hope the educators will walk away with enough knowledge about depression to help someone in their dire time of need.

I commend the Underwoods for what they have done since their son's death. The couple has tried to take a nearly insurmountable tragedy and turn it into something that helps other people, a mark of tremendous courage.

Dan Brannan is editor of the Journal/Tribune and The Messenger.

I felt satisfied we had put our friends' contributions to good use—to promote understanding of depression and to alert people to what to look for and where to go for help. I continued to get notes, e-mails, and phone calls long after the conference was held and that, in fact, is what prompted me to write what I've written here—seeing for the first time just how widespread the need and the problem is in this community alone and, through my reading, all over this country and beyond. There is a great need for information and for shedding light on many of the remaining stigmas and taboos associated with mental illness, depression, and suicide. And, there is a great need on the part of survivors to hear and to understand that they are not alone.

Dr. Kay Redfield Jamison has been a leader in promoting awareness and understanding with her books, *An Unquiet Mind: A Memoir of Moods and Madness*; *Touched with Fire: Manic-Depressive Illness and the Artistic Temperament*; and *Night Falls Fast: Understanding Suicide*. And, she has appeared several times on *Larry King Live* and other shows to help keep the public informed.

For the first time, Dr. David Satcher, Surgeon General of the United States (at the time), made mental illness a top priority for public health. In addition, Vice-President Al Gore's wife, Tipper Gore, has been a leader in the field. Had she become first lady, she would have continued to make depression, suicide, and mental illness a national priority.

Realizing the need to rebuild my life and expand my belief systems and understanding of the world . . . and in an effort to continue to work on myself, I joined *The Institute of Noetic Sciences* (IONS). It was founded by former astronaut Edgar Mitchell to expand consciousness, awareness, and spirituality. Mitchell had had a life-changing experience on an Apollo space mission when he looked out the window of his spaceship and saw the beautiful blue, live planet Earth and suddenly understood there was more to this life and his faith than the narrow church dogma he had learned as a boy growing up. It sparked his desire to know more about others' spiritual paths and beliefs and he wanted to open his mind just as his eyes and heart had opened on his Apollo mission.

I attended IONS' annual meeting, *Spirit in Healing*, in Boca Raton, Florida in mid-July 1996 and heard from Edgar Mitchell and many other speakers who, like Dr. Mitchell, had opened my mind to all the possibilities. I was thrilled to meet in person the British physicist Rupert Sheldrake whose ideas about morphic fields I'd been reading about for some time. I told him, as we stood in line at a buffet dinner, about our very special Samoyed dog, Sasha, and how my husband had rescued her and some of the amazing things she did. He encouraged me to set up video cameras to record her actions so he could include them in his research studies about the special connection there is between humans and their animal companions. There were many other workshops at the conference which were helpful to my healing and self-exploration processes.

My whole world had been turned upside down, and I now knew that apart from the choices we make each day to be good people and to do the right things, we really have very little control over the larger events that occur and can turn our lives around. My career during the previous fifteen years had been in university and higher education strategic planning. Ha! I later heard the now familiar line: If you want to make God laugh, tell him your plans. While it *is* possible to make the choice to try to be as positive as one can and to work toward making goals and dreams come true, believing that doing so ensures any particular outcome ignores all the other forces at work—as well as the context or environment in which one lives and works—which can change everything at any given moment.

For many (perhaps even most) families of those who complete suicide, they are not caught completely unawares because they may have had years to deal with the depressive person and even their previous attempts at suicide. In our case, we had known nothing of any of this. Eric seemed fine to us. Whatever bouts of deep depression he had had (and we learned for the first time in the letter he left us he had had several), he had chosen to keep them to himself. Why? To take care of it himself as the responsible adult (and child) he'd always been? To relieve us of the burden or the worry when we lived so far from him? To not admit, outwardly, to being "mentally ill" because of the stigma attached? To pursue his desire for perfection in being and doing the best he could at everything?

At the time we first learned of his death (having had no clue there'd even been a problem, other than "the usual" down times all of us experience now and then), I thought it was worse not to have ever known because we may have been able to help him and because we'd have done anything we possibly could to help him.

It was only after many years of hearing others' stories—beginning with that survivors' conference in Richmond, Virginia—that we understood that for many families, knowing all along and trying everything they knew how to do to help still made no difference for them in their ability to save their loved one.

For many, attempting suicide is a clear cry for help and attention. It should *always* be taken seriously. For others, especially mature adults like Eric who, as the LAPD officers told us, do not want to be found in time to be saved, their plan is foolproof and final. Their decision made. It is horrifying on the one hand. But Eric's best friend, Shane, said it well at the Clemson service— it's not what he would have wanted for Eric, but he realized he had to respect Eric's choice and learn to accept it. That meant a great deal to us at the time. Shane was helping us to open our eyes to the person he knew in Eric. A person Shane respected and loved. How could we do less than to honor his memory and respect his wish to escape the terrible pain he was in? It was another shock to realize that, as well as we knew Eric and as close as we were to him and as a family, his friend Shane and his wife knew Eric in ways we never did or could. Each life is many lives after all.

CHAPTER THIRTEEN

The Call

Eric loved California. His friends here back home would ask him often when he was coming back to South Carolina. His answer: never. For him, California was where he was meant to be. We could see why. It is a beautiful state and has a great climate. And so much is going on there. So many interesting people. Eric had talked us into leaving South Carolina and planning to move to California when we retired so we could be near him. When we visited him, we would go and look around at various places and eventually, we decided Laguna Beach would be a great spot to retire. That was never to be.

One morning in January 1997, a year and a half from the time Eric died, I was on leave from work and home in bed recovering from foot surgery. I was reading and, quite suddenly, had still another strange experience. *"Go to Mount Shasta,"* I was hearing, clear as a bell. *"Go to Mount Shasta."* I wasn't even sure where Mount Shasta *was!*

Dick brought me an atlas, and I looked it up. The *moment* I saw that it was part of the Cascade chain of mountains located in northern California, I *knew* this was important. And, before the day ended, I knew I would have to go there.

As wild and crazy as it sounded at first, what I understood was that Eric wanted me to take him back to California. That he had never wanted to leave California but was now in South

Carolina (or, his ashes were). And, it was time now for him to go "home." It was he who was asking me to go. I was never more sure of anything in my life. And, hard as it was to do it, I was learning to gather enough courage to *pay attention* rather than give way to people who would scoff at such thinking as mine. Hallucinating, I'm sure they thought. Imagining things. Wishful thinking. I knew better than that. It felt like a test of my own newly forming beliefs to remain true to this strong, compelling "call" I had received.

As I recovered from the surgery, I began doing some research on the mountain. I learned that Mount Shasta is known as a very sacred, very spiritual, mystical place. I had known nothing about it before hearing my call to go there, but now I was learning that it is considered to be one of the most high energy and mystical places on earth. That centuries before, the North American Indians had considered it to be sacred and the center of the universe.

I was eager to go, but by myself? Dick was teaching at the university, and I had a professional conference scheduled that would take me out to California in July, so I thought of adding vacation time to the trip and making my way there then.

But a mountain that is 14,162 feet high? By myself? Insane! I'm not exactly physically fit or an athlete. How would this work? Could I do it even?

As if by magic (or divine guidance), everything began to fall into place. In another amazing synchronicity, someone whom I knew was acquainted with a woman named Mirtala, who happened to be the widow of one of the scientists whose work I had read years before; her husband, Itzhak Bentov, had been, in fact, the first to document the effects of *kundalini* experiences! Mirtala had previously been to a seminar in Mount Shasta, and she was able to recommend the seminar leader as a guide who not only was very familiar with the mountain, he also happened to be a very spiritual man who, she thought, might be willing to help me if I explained about Eric and my reason for going.

I had begun to think of doing a sort of "vision quest" where I would be led to the mountain and then I would spend a couple of days there by myself in contemplation and meditation, in addition to conducting the ceremony for Eric and scattering his ashes there, which would return him to California, as I felt he wished me to do.

The guide was an extremely busy man who traveled a great deal and was away a lot, so it wasn't at all clear any of this was going to work out or even that he would agree to help me. After weeks of near misses, eventually, I was able to contact him to make arrangements and to settle on a date. When he heard my two-day plan, though, he discouraged any idea of my traveling to the mountain alone and planning to stay by myself overnight. Too wild a place, he said, and he wouldn't advise it.

So, I settled for the hours I could have with him and explained the ceremony I wanted to do, the songs I wanted to sing, the poems I planned to read aloud and, when none of that seemed to sound too far-fetched to him at all, that eased my mind. He didn't sound like someone who would try to take over and/or make me feel foolish or self-conscious. He was, after all, still another complete "stranger."

The plans were made, and I was actually going to follow that voice: *Go to Mount Shasta!*

CHAPTER FOURTEEN

Preparations

My mysterious "call" to Mount Shasta remained as powerful as ever while I continued to go to work and make preparations for my travels in July 1997.

It was always clear to me that it was Eric who wanted me to go there, but now I began to have a nagging feeling that there was perhaps more to it than just returning him to California.

Perhaps, because of the circumstances of his death—taking his own life—did he (or, his soul) need my help in some way that wasn't really clear to me? Was he in need of help in order to move on, to pass on to a new life or dimension? Help in putting his soul to rest and making the transition from here to there? Wouldn't it be natural to turn to one's mother for that kind of help? These thoughts became worries and anxiety-ridden questions that began to follow me around, questions about exactly what was being required of me.

As I was now on mailing lists for healing conferences by different groups around the country, I learned of a workshop being held in Cleveland, Ohio, on *Death and Dying*, to be held in June before I was to leave for California. I added a couple of vacation days for a long weekend in search of the help I felt I needed to prepare myself for Mount Shasta.

Fortunately—despite all the time I had had to take off when

we flew to Los Angeles to take care of things and have his funeral there, and then Dick's mother's death—I had the luxury of having accrued enough vacation time to allow me to do these things, due to my twenty-five years of service. In addition, everyone at work was very supportive of me the whole time and wanted to help me in whatever way they could. They all told me that losing a child, especially one's only child, is the most devastating blow a person can have. Many were surprised I was back at work at all.

When I entered the rustic lodge hall where the workshop was being held, I learned that many who were attending were therapists or counselors or psychologists or health-care providers and hospice workers; but many others, like me, were grieving the death of loved ones and looking for help and support with the process. The room immediately felt warm and welcoming.

I felt so grateful to be there and so grateful to have the resources to do it as well as my fully supportive husband who always encouraged me in whatever I felt I wanted or needed to do. Dick's grieving was different from mine, but he seemed to gain comfort from what I was doing and my sharing it with him.

The workshop was led by a wonderful, gentle, very spiritual Jewish man with a background in gestalt therapy. Except for small group exercises, we (some thirty-five of us) sat in a wide circle on the floor. Many had drums with them for some of the prayers and songs that were part of a group that met "in circle" on a regular basis. Everyone was very friendly and helpful. *"When the student is ready, the teacher appears"* as the saying goes, and that felt right to me. It seemed as though whenever I most needed help since Eric died, in one way or another, help would appear . . . would be provided. My belief in a living, loving universe continued to prove true.

Among the many strange things that were happening to me— some of which I've already mentioned—one was still another mysterious but clear message from Eric, I believed, about a Siberian shaman and his Samoyed dog. At the time, I had no idea the

meaning of this particular message. At first I thought he might
be giving me an idea for a children's story or something. I really
had *no idea* what it meant, just that it was very, very powerful
and very clear. I didn't even know what a "shaman" was at the
time. I knew very little about Siberia, and all I knew about
Samoyeds was what little I'd read after we'd rescued our dog,
Sasha, and brought her home to live with us when she was a
year-and-a-half old in May 1990.

The Samoyed people were nomads dating centuries back to
Siberia and they relied upon their fluffy white dogs with the
dark eyes and ever-present smiles as sled dogs, as well as to help
them herd their reindeer and to give them warmth on freezing
winter nights.

Somehow, there was a connection here, and Eric was trying
to help me make it and to understand something that transcended
the boundaries of our own life story together.

It was both mystifying and exciting at the same time, feelings
that were to follow me in the days (and years) to come.

This message about the Siberian shaman and his Samoyed
dog had been with me in the early months after Eric died in
1995, so it was by now quite familiar to me and would crop up
now and then in things I read or in information coming in. Very
mysterious. Quite haunting. Powerful! What did it mean?

I had, as I've said, always been a voracious reader, so adding
books to read on Siberia and on shamanism added a new
dimension to my explorations. Shamans, I learned, were religious
figures dating back centuries who were believed to have the power
to heal the sick and to communicate with spirits of the dead and
with the world beyond. They were found primarily in northern
Asia (though later many were in South America, Australia, and
elsewhere around the world) and among Ural-Altaic (including
Samoyed) peoples in Siberia (in the former Soviet Union).

It was a bit overwhelming to stand back and consider that,
along with my *kundalini* experiences opening me to new spiritual

dimensions, I was also receiving powerful messages about ancient spiritual people including these connected somehow to our beloved Samoyed dog Dick had rescued in 1990, just as Eric was graduating from Vanderbilt University and preparing to move across the country and begin a new life.

It seemed an unmistakable message of connection and transcendence of boundaries of time and space, just as I'd been studying in the new sciences and chaos theory at the time. Doors were being opened to me, I felt sure of that.

With all this bubbling up inside me, when I had learned earlier that the Omega conference people in upstate New York would be holding a workshop in June before my trip to Mount Shasta with a real Siberian shaman, Grandfather Misha Duvan who was in his nineties, I took it as a clear sign that I was to go there and see what I could learn from him. Unfortunately, he died just before the workshop in New York was to take place, so the one *On Death and Dying* in Cleveland, Ohio seemed to be the right alternative.

In Cleveland that weekend, I made friends with a number of people and in particular a woman, a librarian, whose husband had died only a month before. We felt an instant rapport and continued to keep in touch for a couple of years following the workshop.

During one of the exercises, we were instructed to close our eyes, meditate and visualize an image—whatever came to us— and then draw it. I had a strange and surprising intuition as I drew mine that it was being given to me by Grandfather, the Siberian shaman. It was a sort of fractal image, like reindeer antlers or the outline of a river as seen from an airplane or on a map and, when we began sharing with one another, while talking, you can imagine my great shock when my new friend reached into her handbag and pulled out a red scarf that had been buried inside and that I had never seen before. It was covered with the *same* image I had just received! Exactly the same image! Again, there are no coincidences, I believe, so this message from the universe, this amazing synchronicity, had come, I believed, to reassure me that I was not imagining things—that I was making some important connections which were being reinforced.

As if that weren't enough, when we broke for lunch, my friend was busy with some people she knew, so I went through the buffet line and wandered outside feeling happy to be by myself and to be quiet with the thoughts swirling around inside me.

I had also had a powerful journey during one meditation in which I had seen Eric bathed in a golden light sitting cross-legged, smiling, at the bottom of the ocean, surrounded by beautiful, colorful sea life. He had always loved the ocean and we had gone there every year since he was two, to vacation at the coast. He definitely seemed happy and in a good place in my visualization of him.

As I said, the workshop was held in a rural setting; we were surrounded by woods and meadows. I wandered outside, with my plate, and went over to a picnic table where there was just one other woman. Soon, we began to talk as we shared our meal.

She was a hospice worker and—before I had told her *any part* of my own story—she talked about her young son and about how they had *added another member to their family, an exchange student who was from* . . . Siberia! Somewhat breathlessly, I asked if she remembered *where* he was from, what town, what body of water, forest, or mountains nearby?

I was ASTONISHED to hear her name the exact same town and area that I had visualized back at home a few days before leaving town as I had meditated on the possible meaning of Eric's message about the Siberian shaman and his Samoyed dog! INCREDIBLE! How could this really be happening? What was its meaning for me? What was I meant to do with this information?

I came to see these messages and experiences as affirmations from the world beyond to show that there *is* more than just our more narrow frame of reference and consciousness in our lives. Life *is* eternal and there are many, many dimensions and much beyond our simple "reality-based" worlds which are so focused on our external and material existence and interests.

All that science reading I had felt driven to do so many years before made much more sense to me now. My working world was a scientific university setting. To make sense of things, I was trained that one must explore the science(s) behind them. Anything less lacked credibility. Before experiencing what I was going through now, I would need to have satisfied myself that I had a foundation and some understanding of the science of how things work in the world. Then and only then could I allow myself the freedom to go beyond those boundaries and consider what else may be there.

Niels Bohr's principle of complementarity had especially, as I've said, always spoken to me. Like the two sides of a coin—just because you can only see one side at a time doesn't mean that the other side is not there . . . does not exist! Exactly!

Just because I can no longer see Eric now and touch him or prove what has happened since his death doesn't mean his spirit is not in fact here and very much alive.

Another of my favorite scientists, Rupert Sheldrake whom I mentioned earlier, also helped me put things such as these into perspective for me:

He pointed out that there are trillions of galaxies in the cosmos, each with a billion stars, each of these with a fifteen billion-year history. Ninety to ninety-nine percent of matter is still unknown to us! Most of life *is* in fact a mystery. There is MUCH we don't know yet. Anything IS possible! Why, it even seems quite arrogant to believe otherwise.

Now, with these new experiences, I was able to leave the Cleveland workshop with some powerful experiences that told me I *was* on the right track—keep going!

CHAPTER FIFTEEN

The Mountain

As July grew closer and my trip to Mount Shasta was coming up, I began to feel both apprehensive and excited at the same time. I began having pains in my stomach which the doctor, who had helped me get my high blood pressure stabilized the year before, told me was likely an ulcer.

Dr. C. asked me if I had had any added stress at work, and I told him no, I wasn't aware of any. When I told him it was important to me to get this problem healed before my trip and explained what I had planned, he asked me, *"And you don't think it is THE most stressful thing of all to have lost your only child and to be planning to go out into the wilderness and climb a mountain by yourself?"*

I could see he was right and realized my newly increased awareness of so much happening to me apparently didn't extend to awareness about my own body and the effects these events were having on it.

But who could not be excited? The more I read about Mount Shasta, the more intrigued I became about what I might find there.

Mount Shasta, I learned, is the southern point of the Cascade

Range of mountains. Geologists call it Cascadia, a chain of volcanic mountains with intense fires burning beneath them (also known as the Pacific Ring of Fire) that includes Mounts Shasta, St. Helens, and Rainier, and stretches in an 800-mile arc in the Pacific Northwest across three states (California, Oregon, and Washington) marking the slow, grinding descent of an oceanic fragment of Earth's outer shell beneath North America through a process called subduction. Cascadia begins about 200 miles north of San Francisco and ends along the north coast of Vancouver Island in British Columbia.

Mount Shasta is the highest mountain in the Cascade Range at 14,162 feet and remains snow-capped all year long. Its snowy peak can be seen from 200 miles away. Mount Shasta is a sixteen million-year-old now dormant volcano which last erupted in 1786 and is believed to erupt every 200 to 300 years. It was first climbed in 1854.

Many view it as a spiritual energy vortex, a fountainhead of cosmic energy; the mountain was and still is considered by many Native American Indian tribes to be the center of the universe. Many still hold ceremonies on its slopes every year.

In some examples, in 1989 it was the site of a Tibetan Fire Ceremony, an international gathering point, and earlier, in August 1987 it was the site of the Harmonic Convergence which was part of a worldwide event—along with other global communication events such as Hands Across America, Space Bridges, and World Peace Day—which were intended to herald a new phase of world cooperation and harmony among the planet's peoples and its environment. According to the literature, Mount Shasta was chosen for these events because it was considered among the most sacred mountains on earth. Nearly five thousand people, from as far away as Australia and Europe, gathered above Panther Meadows to greet the sunrise and to conduct their ceremonies and events.

Oh, the history of this majestic mountain! I had known none of it before I had had that mysterious "call" to go there! It felt astonishing to learn all this, as though on some level, at some other time, I, or we, had had a history there.

It was especially intriguing to read *after* my visit there—after I arrived home with various books I'd bought there—of the early Russian explorers who had settled in the area in the early nineteenth century who may have been instrumental in discovering Mount Shasta. In 1812 they had first sent a number of expeditions and trapping brigades up the small coastal rivers in the area. In 1841, one Russian climbed Mt. Saint Helena, a sister mountain in the Cascades and placed a plaque there naming it in honor of Empress Helena of Russia. Mount Shasta and others can be seen from Mount St. Helens, so historians surmise the Russians saw it, hence, the name "Shasta." The Russian word for "white," or "pure," is *tchastal.*

As I read about all this, long after my *"calling to"* and my own visit there, I realized with astonishment that I had been drawn to the mountain chain once before! I had had a professional meeting in Oregon in April 1985 and, as I often do, I had added some vacation days at the time so I could see the area. On a whim (or was it more than that? I wondered now), I had decided to charter a plane, quite inexpensively, to fly over Mount St. Helens which had erupted in April 1980.

I had been fascinated when I followed that story at the time, and I wanted to see it for myself. It was a fantastic flight, quite exhilarating as it was a small plane and our pilot swooped down right over the crater so we could take photographs and see the whole mountain. It was one of those once-in-a-lifetime experiences. And now, as I look back, I don't recall having seen Mount Shasta from that vantage point, but perhaps I *was* being drawn back there?

Perhaps on some deeper level I was very much aware, all these years later, that this was a very special place where my son would feel at home? I wondered. A woman with established psychic powers had told me, not long after Eric died, that in ancient times Eric had traveled widely and was accompanied by a white wolf. A white wolf! (Sasha, I had immediately thought to myself!) How could she have known of that connection? Had Eric wanted to return to his home? His home long before his lifetime with us? A place very familiar to him? All part of the Mystery.

The old part of me with the long-entrenched but much more narrow belief system almost automatically rejected such thinking. Where was the science to back up such beliefs? And yet, the new part of me that was being opened up to a much larger view of the world, the universe, the cosmos . . . the part of me that had been struck, inexplicably and unmistakably, by *"lightning"* and then was charged through and through with *kundalini* energy . . . the part of me that found one incredible synchronicity after another occurring . . . the part of me that had always believed in endless possibilities . . . told me there was so much more, and that I would do well to pay close attention to all these events and connections. To not so automatically reject experiences that felt, and were, so real to me. Messages were being given to me. Information was being introduced to me. To reject all these would be, it seemed to me, nothing short of the worst kind of ingratitude, a sort of sacrilege.

Many people besides me had obviously experienced some of these strange things happening to them as well. For Mount Shasta alone, there had been, for many decades, legends of eerie phenomena and mystical beings showing up. Perhaps because fewer than a third of the thousand climbers a year ever make it to its ice-packed summit, the mountain was symbolic of the mysterious, the unknown.

Reading all this later—after returning home—I recalled what little I had read and known *before* I left home and realized my excitement and turmoil (including my stomach problems, not to mention my blood pressure!) probably couldn't have stood flying in there knowing all that at the time! I was already astonished and overwhelmed as it was just at the idea of feeling "called" there to help my son somehow. If I had put *all* this together all at once, if I had made all these connections then, I may not have withstood it! Just thinking to myself as I prepared: this is real! This is actually going to happen! was more than enough to take in.

I decided these things were happening to me to give me hope—the hope Eric had lost—and to keep me going. To lead me to an understanding of the vast dimensions of "reality." To restore my faith and my desire to go on living.

All my life it seemed I had been one who was able to see "the big picture" (thus, I was told, making me a natural for a career in strategic planning), and now I was being called upon to open my eyes to non-ordinary reality and to other dimensions as well. Could all this be true? How could I deny what continued to happen? How could I deny or reject such important life experiences? My whole life changed when my son died, and this was part of it. This was information I had come here to learn and to know. I felt a growing sense of humility in the face of what just happened to be *All That Is.*

CHAPTER SIXTEEN

In Mount Shasta

Arriving at the small airport in Redding, California, the largest town closest to Mount Shasta, I had decided against renting a car after having talked, back home in South Carolina, to someone who lived there and told me that being unfamiliar with the area, and as wild as it was there, one wrong turn off the beaten path could spoil my whole trip—that there were wild animals and such and it was not exactly a good idea for a woman traveling alone (who had no sense of direction!) to venture off on her own. I was told there would be a taxi at the airport that could get me to the cabin where I was staying.

As it turned out, that taxi company for Mount Shasta (one person with a four-wheel drive) had just gone out of business the weekend before I arrived. I finally managed to talk a Redding-area taxi driver into taking me the whole way there, about an hour and a half's drive away, uphill, towards the mountain. It was more than two hours from the airport to get there since the driver got lost. I watched as the meter ticked on to $150 but realized that I didn't have much choice now that I was there and it would soon be nightfall.

About an hour into our drive, the driver told me to watch out the window, that Mount Shasta would soon loom into view. He had to stop for gas (he did at least stop the meter then!), so I was able to get out and breathe in the cool mountain air and marvel at the wonder of Mount Shasta's snowy majesty.

What a glorious place! My heart was racing. It was really true. I was really here! Oh, Eric, I thought, my dear, sweet Eric. I was awed by what it was that brought me here. I had never *heard* of Mount Shasta when Eric called me there. How amazing this all was! I was filled with both anxiety and anticipation at the same time. I wanted this to be just right. For Eric. The whole purpose of this trip and all it took to get here was to bring Eric back home and, in some mysterious way I still felt unsure about, to help him.

That night, after talking to Dick and checking with the guide to let him know I had arrived and to pin down the details about our departure time for the mountain, I fell into an exhausted but happy sleep.

As the time we could meet and do the ceremony was planned for another day, I had the next day to myself to explore the area and to go through the ceremony and prepare. Again, I learned it had been a bad idea not to have rented a car, and after a few phone calls, I had a car to drive around town and to various places close by at the foothills of the mountain.

The town itself was small and had a special charm to it because the people were so friendly and laid back. It reminded me of towns in the upper peninsula of Michigan or in Norway, where Dick and I had visited when we had lived in Europe early in our marriage.

One thing was inescapable—the town was dominated by the majesty of the mountain there before you as you drove around or walked out of a store or wandered around. To look up and see that magnificent sight was so exciting it set my heart pounding whenever I saw it.

Although it was July, I was surprised at how hot it was in town. I followed the Everitt Memorial Highway and drove out to the Mount Shasta Ski Bowl. I was thrilled to ride the ski lift up and up and sit there in that open chair lift and drink in the glory and beauty of it. Very spiritual, very mystical, and I really felt Eric very close by the whole time, smiling at me.

I drove back into town and explored some fascinating bookstores, bought some groceries, and drove back to my cabin to lay out my plans for the ceremony the next day.

As I went over my poems and songs, I felt uneasy for some reason and decided I should do a deep meditation. I lit a candle, said a prayer of thanks, closed my eyes and before long, felt astonished to be seeing clearly, Grandfather come walking out from behind a stand of tall pine trees and sit down in a nearby clearing.

He asked me if I had remembered to include the image (the one he'd given me earlier at the workshop). Oh, dear! I had not! And then I saw Eric come walking out from behind those same trees, smiling, as he sat down next to Grandfather!

What I understood from Eric (without words) was that he wanted me to eliminate one of the poems, *The Spiral*, a sad one I had written about a mother's anguish at losing him, and instead, he wanted a new poem, one about his friends and all the people who had loved him. This was to be a celebration of all that was good and happy, not a ceremony of grief and loss. And, I should remember to speak about the Mountain, he said.

I felt jolted and electrified by these messages. They were so clear! So specific! Eric wanted me to know what he wanted for the ceremony! Astounding. Without question this had come from somewhere beyond my own thinking and imagination. I had *forgotten*, was unaware, of the missing piece in this ceremony that had made no mention of his friends and loved ones! I felt so happy, so excited, so overwhelmed.

I took out a sheet of paper first, drew a circle or *mandala* and within it, re-created the image—the fractal-like, riverlike (as seen from above), reindeer-antlerlike image Grandfather had asked about.

Then in my folder, I searched for the sad poem Eric wanted

me to discard and began writing the new one, with tears streaming. I wrote another about the mountain and sat re-reading, uncertain I had covered everything adequately.

I decided to read them aloud and call on Eric to decide for me. As I did this, the candle flame began flickering wildly, wildly, though there was no breeze whatsoever in the room, and though my own breath was not at all in the direction of, or anywhere near, the flame.

Eric? Eric, is that you? More flickering. Distinctly answering! Is this right, son? Is this what you want for tomorrow? More flickering. No question in my mind! This was an answer to my question, and I was to understand that it was so. It stopped flickering after answering.

Even I questioned for a moment whether this was just wishful thinking. But in my heart I knew it was not. Eric's spirit was, indeed, present. Was indeed aware. Was indeed guiding me. I had asked for help and help was being given. Not so surprising, really. If you believe in a living, loving universe. If you believe in dimensions beyond material reality. If you believe a mother's love and concern for her son and a son's for his mother.

I carefully and neatly copied over the new poems I'd scribbled earlier and added them to the other, carefully typed ones in my folder.

I packed my little bag for the next day and fell into a happy, contented sleep.

CHAPTER SEVENTEEN

The Ceremony

The next morning I awoke with great anticipation and some anxiety. After getting ready, I lit the candle and sat quietly in prayer and meditation until the guide knocked on my door.

I invited him in and was glad he seemed to be a kind, friendly man who listened willingly as I went over my plans with him and agreed we could do this just as I wished.

He had a four-wheel drive vehicle, necessary to handle the rough terrain he'd be driving through, and we set off chatting away and getting acquainted as we drove on up to the mountain.

He told me that even though it was July, eight inches more snow had fallen overnight at the top of the mountain, and that many climbers came here attempting to reach the top, but many were unprepared for what they'd find. A few people had died in the attempt in past years.

I felt happy and secure to be traveling with him. He knew the area and the mountain intimately and had spent a great deal of time on it over the years. He took some off-the-beaten-path roads over and through the thick forest area, in a path right between the trees. As we climbed further, he pointed out an avalanche area that had killed several people the previous winter.

He told me we were going to an area called Upper Panther

Meadow, an area considered sacred by the Indian tribes and by others who revered the mountain.

Once he parked the car, we had quite a hike to get there, and when I lagged behind, he took my bag from me to ease my load.

We arrived at an utterly enchanting place where the volcano eruption hundreds and thousands of years before had lifted the rocks and spilled out the lava. There were tiny, colorful wildflowers everywhere, growing up between the rocks; there were also tiny mushrooms, and a small stream was bubbling and trickling beneath our feet.

He told me that for a part of the walk to get to the area he'd chosen for the ceremony, I should take notice that there would be no birds flying there as they did not enter that sacred area. It was exactly as he had said, birds flying, singing, and then suddenly, nothing for quite a stretch, only for the birds to reappear later, beyond that particular area. Most mysterious. Enchanting. My heart was pounding. I couldn't believe it. I was here! This was really happening! *Oh, thank you, God,* was my small, humble prayer.

I was *astonished* when I saw that the area he had chosen for the ceremony—an outcropping of rock, a shelf, with wildflowers and flowing water beneath with a clearing and some tall pine trees—looked *exactly* like the trees and area I had seen Grandfather and Eric walking out from the night before! Incredible!

I was very pleased, as I set up the small altar area with candles, pictures, and other things I'd brought, to find that our guide had opened his briefcase and had taken out a long purple satin ribbon or vestment and put it around his neck. He took out an ornate gold chalice, poured some wine, which we shared, and set it on the altar.

I began with a prayer of thanks to God and to the Mountain and then proceeded to sing the songs and to read aloud my poems. Now and then he would comment affirmatively, *"Eric would like that, Mom. He is proud of you."* At one point, I even blew some bubbles, the kind one buys for children, because one of my dearest friends and her small boys had asked me to. As the bubbles glistened in the sunlight, the guide exclaimed, *"Way to go, Eric! Now you're sparkling on a mountain breeze."*

I handed him the small, ornate pewter container of Eric's ashes; we said a prayer, and then he began circling three pine trees (I hadn't told him of my vision the night before!), saying aloud a prayer, talking to Eric, to the other spirits there, and dedicating this area to Eric and his spirit so he would find peace in being there while he spread his ashes all around the area. He brought the container back to me, so I could add my own words for Eric as I spread the remainder of the ashes. He said this was long considered to be a very sacred place with many other friendly spirits there to keep Eric good company. He would not be alone.

I wept for joy; it was all so perfect, far beyond anything I'd even imagined or hoped it would be. We were careful to return everything exactly as we had found it, out of respect for the mountain, and we packed up our things to leave.

On our walk back, I felt overwhelmed with gratitude and humbled by the whole experience. We did it, Eric. We did it. Now you're home again. Back in your beloved California.

As we reached the car and drove away, chatting about the day and how wonderful Eric was, I felt that my call, the one I'd heard so clearly back in January, had been fulfilled, had been completed.

I was wrong.

CHAPTER EIGHTEEN

Eric's Message

The terrain was pretty rough and rugged up where we were and as we bumped over the ground and through the trees to get to the road, the guide pointed out the different kinds of trees and vegetation and told me stories about the area.

As we got onto a narrow road heading back down the mountain, I was startled to see a huge, magnificent hawk swoop down straight toward us. I turned and exclaimed, *"Oh my, this means something, don't you think?"* He agreed and for some reason, immediately swung the car around on that narrow mountain road and circled back.

Suddenly, shockingly, right before us, up in the air above our heads, above the car, a tiny bird in mid-flight plummeted to the earth. We gasped in awe and just looked at one another. Incredible. He stopped the car, got out, and went over and picked up the bird and brought it back and laid the tiny, still warm body in my hands. It was a beautiful, brilliantly colored yellow goldfinch.

"I've seen this happen only once before," he said. *"You know what this death means, don't you?"* *"No! No!"* I said, feeling upset.

"She has sacrificed her life so you can have yours back again. It means she has given you back your life."

Instantly, with tears streaming, I understood. I had worried so much before coming here that Eric's spirit needed help in some way and that although I didn't understand what it was I was to do to help him, I had decided to go there and return him at least to his beloved California. But now it was clear that it was much more than that. Eric could not find peace until I let him go. His *"unfinished business"* had been ME!

Somehow, I knew this suddenly with absolute certainty, just as if he had spoken it aloud to me. Because he couldn't do it himself, the hawk and goldfinch were messengers of the universe who were sure to get my attention before I left that mountain, believing I had done all there was to do.

In a beautiful, powerful, otherworldly way, Eric's message was clear:

> Life is eternal.
> I am here.
> I am fine.
> But I can't
> find peace
> until you do.
>
> Your life
> must go on.
>
> I am here,
> and I love you.

EPILOGUE

I brought my tiny goldfinch home, and on August 10, 1997, two years to the day of Eric's death, I lit some candles, and we held a little ceremony to bury her, inside a beautiful, blue, crystal glass box, out beneath the young oak tree in our backyard overlooking the lake, marked by a hanging plaque I had found that reads:

> *Each soul must meet*
> *the morning sun*
> *the new sweet earth*
> *and the Great Silence*
> *alone.*
>
> (Lakota Indian)

The year before on his birthday, June 3, we had planted the tree and held a little ceremony as we'd scattered some of his ashes there so he could rest in peace. Now perhaps he can.

A SELECTION
OF POEMS
for my son

His Mother's Lament

O pain of Death
why can't I find
that Time has come
to clear at last
your ruin from
my smoldering,
deep-poker'd heart
whose scars now mark
the love I'd thought
would never ever
leave me cold
 or in the dark
again.

October 1995

Full Circle

In my twenty-seventh year I was
when you were born . . .
in twenty-seven hours' labor.

Twenty-seven years of Life
you had!
Twenty-seven days, my cycle.
(On you I'd hung the moon.)

Like you, it's left me now.
I'm done.

November 1995

GAIA

At last I hear
your prayer for me,
Mother.

And here within
these outstretched arms
so full of color,
love, and light
I've learned
that Death
is not
a dreadful ending.

It is a floating free
return to you.
A loving promise
of beginning.

November 1996

Eric

Just now, my son,
my memory's served me,
and my dreams
are much more real
than the "real world"
daylight images
will henceforth
need to be.

I fly with Eagle
soaring, swooping
over snowcapped mountains,
gliding over plains
of thundering herds
and hear their hooves
and heartbeats
in my chest,
and in that moment
I am them!

And when
the shaman's drum
pulls my spirit
into breathing
in your soul
and spirit,
is that, too,

an image
from a dream
or now a memory of
what is real?

And when
by firelight
I join you
in a dance
of soul and spirit
in a vision
I now have of you,
perhaps our memory's alive
in Dreamtime
and is that vision
from so long ago,
anima mundi.

May 24, 1997

" . . . *this world is indeed a living being
endowed with a soul and intelligence . . . a single
living entity containing all other living entities,
which by their nature are related.*"

—Plato, Fourth Century B.C.

Your New Life

I'm here with you,
my son.
I'm here.

And when you feel
the time has come,
lift up, fly free,
dear son, on into
your new life.

Remember.
Remember and deny
Man's hate,
his loneliness,
despair.

Forever carry with you
deep remembrance of
this Love and Light
by whose embrace
you Know now.

Remember it
as candle flame
(your soul),
and together we will
breathe and blow
eternal Spirit's
warmth and love,

to light, to cheer
each day of
your new life.

Remember!
Fly fearlessly,
sweet boy.

Be filled with joy
and hope renewed
to carry you
on into, through,
this miracle . . .
your new life!

(I'll remember, too.)

July 2, 1997

144

Handwritten in Mount Shasta the night before the ceremony, July 6, 1997 (at Eric's request)

We Honor Them

Sweet boy,
your life
was filled
with love
and laughter
and good friends.
We honor them,
and you,
today.

Young man,
so good,
you've known
of love
and ecstasy,
true happiness
and bliss.
We honor them,
and you,
today.

Dear Eric,
your father,
sweet Sasha,
and your family
all love you so.
We honor them,
and you,
today.

Your life
was very full . . .
To all of us,
great Gift.

Godspeed,
sweet soul.
Godspeed!

July 6, 1997

The Mountain

Mount Shasta,
we have heard
your call.
We're here.
We thank you.

All your beauty,
all your majesty
hold secrets
and great mystery.

We have heard
your call.
We're here.
We thank you.

Within you lies
the soul
of God
and all of us.

We have heard
your call.
We're here.
We thank you.

July 6, 1997

(This is the poem Eric asked me to eliminate from the ceremony because it was too sad and he wanted the ceremony to be a celebration of his life.)

The Spiral

Behold the
spiral galaxy
of death
alive.

For him
spun down
the depths
of sound,
of fire,
cold.

For him
the upward flights
of freedom,
spirit,
soul.

His mother lives
forever spinning,
spiraling
up and down
in sad forever search
of him
in galaxies
unknown.

February 20, 1997

For you, Golden Bird

Majestically, Hawk swooped in to us,
a signal:
Pay attention.
Something's coming.

*"Oh my, this means something,
don't you think?"*
He nodded, and on that rugged,
narrow mountain road
swung the car around,
and circled back.

And, there before us
instantly
you appeared,
high above us
and . . . you died!
And dropped down
to the ground.

We gasped in awe
and looked at one another,
disbelieving witnesses
to a sacred sacrifice.

"I've seen this happen
only once before," he said,
and, bending down,
he brought you to me
and lay your
tiny, still-warm body,
brilliant gold
into my palm.

(*"Oh, a goldfinch!"* . . . *me*)
And he said,
"You know what this death
means, don't you?"
No! No!

"She died for you.
It means she's given back
your life. You have your
life back now."

(In my grief, I'd come here to
the highest sacred meadows
of Mount Shasta
with the ashes of my son.)

Then through my tears
I realized,
Dear God! All my anguish,
all my worry for his soul —
Eric's 'unfinished business'
. . . has been ME!

Oh, how could this be?
Could this really be
happening to me?

Driving back down that
narrow mountain road,
having done the ceremony,
Hawk and Goldfinch
were sent (he said)
as messengers to me
. . . from the Universe
. . . and Eric.

You have a new life now.
It's time to put the past
behind you.
Try your wings.

The world is new.
You have new eyes to see.
You have new work to do.
And, you have Me.

August 10, 1997

The Labyrinth at
Grace Cathedral
San Francisco

Heart pounding
I entered the labyrinth —
the one outdoors,
the one circled with trees.

Birds rising,
circling, and singing,
and in my head,
music of my own:

On a clear day
rise and look around you
and you'll see
who you are.
On a clear day
how it will astound you . . . .
Well, we'll see, I thought.)

Surprised to find
I had that path
all to myself,
I circled 'round
and soon I found
right beside me
a tall young man

so like my son,
beginning his walk.

In and out,
in and out,
we'd weave
around it.
At times it seemed
he'd gone.
But then he'd reappear.
Only to disappear
again.

Like life and death
I thought,
with stinging tears.

It's only now,
months later,
that I've realized . . . .

I had found it so hard
to leave
that sacred place,
so I'd lingered
on a bench nearby
listening to music,
a meditation:
"Return to the Mother"
(it happened to be!).

No one had come
to the labyrinth,
so I was alone.
Until the young man
came back.

Like me
he'd wanted
to walk it
himself,
alone.

Like me
he was
searching . . .
still.

And so,
he chose
to
come
back.

July 1997

January 7, 1998

Small, eight-pound babe
a mother holds
in arms enfolding,
holding. Holding.

At LA's airport
three years ago,
at six feet four
(age twenty-six)
he held his mother
(five feet four)
in arms enfolding.
Holding.

"Bye. Be Good.
I love you. Call me."
It was the last time
I would see him.

This pillow
he has left behind
is small.
In my arms, enfolded,
I hold it close
to close
the hole left
in my heart
that tunnels
to forever,
to wherever
he is now.

Oh, sweet babe,
come let me
hold you.
Hold me.

I didn't know!
I didn't know!

Marlene's Gift

My life
was plagued
with fear
and doubt.
My son
was dead,
by his
own hand.

Despair!
And oh,
the Pain.
Thoughts
and wishes
for my Death . . .
escape.

Amazingly,
blazingly,
spared.
There's work
to do.

How? I'm
going mad.
Quite mad
with grief.
And, something
else
(the work
to do.)

So, in you came
from somewhere
in the Universe.

"Eric's laughing,"
you said.
"He's with his grandfather.
They are laughing.
They seem
happy together."

You could see that.
And him.
And in an instant,
the veil
was lifted.
In an instant,
new worlds
appeared.

And, hope.
And, will.
There's work
to do.
The work
to do
(the amazing Mystery.)

The amazing Marlene.

March 1998

158

Seasoned

You could have
drowned alone
at three,
in a blue-green pool
of summer, son.
It happens.

In the crisp, cool air
of autumn's light
children in costumes
plunge their faces,
laughing
into a pool
of reddened apples.
Imperfect prize.
Choice.

Remember that stranding
winter's storm
when you and friends
played like children
in the snow
then warmed yourselves inside
with fire, food, and love?
Choice.

A quarter century plus
of memory smiles
and seasons.
Then you drowned
alone
in a dark-red pool
of your own.
Choice.

Can you hear that baby wailing?
The deafening sounds
of siren-blackened night?
Oh. The wailing is my own.

The water's cool and soothing.
Soothes the shock of verdant
spring.
Silent. Dark. And deep,
Unfailing. Breathe.
Breathe, and let it go.

May 7, 1998

LAMENTS

June 5, 1968
June 5, 1998

When you were born
thirty years ago
my joy
was boundless.

I didn't want
to hear the news
as I cradled you
then, at three days old,
that Robert Kennedy
was dead.

You were born!
That's all I knew
and all I'd hear.
You were alive
and all was well
in my new world
with you.

And now the world
commemorates
these thirty years
since Bobby died,
and everyone
remembers him.

But what of you
now nearly
three years dead?

The world has lost,
will never know,
what each of you
could do.

Eric

These days and nights
are all
the same
without you.

No matter what
we try to do
still, we are
without you.

And everywhere
we try to go
we come back home
without you.

The road ahead
looms into view
and here we are
without you.

I thought the pain
would ease with time.
Instead it's changed
into a life
without you.

January 16, 1999

Anniversary

As the anniversary
of your Death draws
near again,
my son,
what have I learned from you?
Why did you come to me?

As your child,
to teach you
how to listen
to your inner Self.
And me. To know me.
To know God.
And, immortality.

To lift, to fly,
to look above horizons
to the skies,
the Universe,
the stars . . .
the more there is
than this. And us
alone.

To leave the pain
and suffering
behind . . .
at last.
At least.

To find your way
outside your Self,
to go inside,
within.
Like me, to find
the Universe is ours.
And, has ever been.

July 30, 1999

Sasha, Proud Samoyed

b. Nov. 12, 1988, d. Oct. 15, 1999

Your sweet and gentle spirit's
spread throughout the house
into every corner,
heart, and soul.

Now you're gone,
I close my eyes
and see yours
here before me:
deep, bright, almond brown,
rimmed in black,
tracing back
the centuries.

And I recall so long ago,
in southwest Siberia,
the Samoyed people,
your family then;
who loved it, too,
whenever you
would smile at them.

All day you worked
so hard and happily,
a shepherd to their reindeer herds,
a lead to pull their sleds.

And in the icy Arctic nights
your silky, snow-white fur
drawn close
gave in comfort,
warmth, and love,
defeat against the chill.

And on those nights
when shamans drummed
and danced by firelight
you sat in circle,
sharing sounds and song
and secrets
you still know
until this day.

Our smiling Sasha,
you are
ever near.

October 18, 1999

The Holidays
—without you

At first it was
impossible.

Impossible to imagine
—to think—
of celebrating
holidays
without you.

Thanksgiving.
Christmas.
The New Year
(and now, a new millennium)
without you here.
Impossible.

The table laden . . .
all your favorites.
We give thanks . . .
. . . your place
is empty
(so are we).
Impossible.

The air is filled
with music . . .
Christmas carols
you loved to hear.
The lighted tree,

the decorations,
warmth and cheer,
the special gifts:
your favorite
time of year.
For us:
another year
without you here.
Impossible!

Then soon
we'd raise a glass
to toast
"the future" . . .
a New Year
without you here.
Impossible.

And then . . .
the years'
slow winding
down,
the carriage
past
impossible.

And we,
like alchemists
of old,
try to turn
the dull, deep
ache and emptiness
into the golden,
happy memories

of all those years
we had with you.

Remembering
what we've learned:
your legacy and life
have always been
to teach us
what is
possible.

December 5, 1999

August 10, 2000

Five Years
(Haiku)

The howling, screaming

silence quiets down to breath.

Breathe in. Earth. And, you.

Mother's Day

To show me you are here,
when searching for a pad to write
my thoughts tonight,
the one I found held my notes of a
long conversation as we talked
on the phone years ago.
About your working on *Gump*,
a new girl you were dating,
a movie you'd seen,
bills you'd paid . . .
catching me up on all your news.
Pages and pages
of you.

I used to do that.
Scribble while you talked
so I could tell Dad later
and savor the memories for
myself. I missed you,
living so far away.
(I still do.)

The pad I grabbed tonight.
The pen from among so many
just happened to be *"Mount Shasta,
California"* with the mountain
drawn on it.

Imagine that. Both together.
Speaking to me.

The whole world is alive
with you.

This much I know.

May 7, 2001

The World As I Know It Now

When I heard
the latest theory
that the Universe
is expanding after all . . .
is picking up speed,
that made sense to me,
given my new reality.

Billions and billions
of galaxies and stars
and vast quantities
of dark, unknown
energy and space,
"the vast unknown."

So like the vast void
of life without you
these six years,
sweet son,
strangely encompassing
a deep, inner *knowing* of
many dimensions,
many lives,
many realities.
Knowing within unknown.

My world too
seems so divided
between those who know

174

and explore all
the Universe holds . . .
and those who have
no real wish to know
(understandably so).

And though I look up
to the stars
and see your smiling face
and you are there
(as well as ever here),
still I long to hold you
and hear you laugh out loud.
For real.

There is
that which
one can know
and never know.
And there is
that which
one can have
and not have.
For now.

August 10, 2001

Haiku on
Losing My Breast

The worst that could hap-
pen to us already has.
Our son, Eric, died.

February 9, 2002

Year Seven

In the still quiet
of the morning son
your bright warm Spirit
fills the room
and me
with energy,
to greet another day,
glad to be alive.
(How could that be?)

You said we would survive
and we have,
miracle of miracles
happening every day
who knows why.

August 10, 2002

In My Heart

"When you're down and out
lift up your head and shout.
It's going to be a great day . . . ."
. . . words to a song
I'd long forgotten.

Music,
language of the
Spheres.

What a marvel
that in the
Human Soul
struggling
to go on,
struggling
to survive

there is still
a song
to save us
(happy even).

August 2002

Messages

Today I heard the
story of a mother,
just like me,
who each year
dreaded when
her son's
Death day
came around
again.

She would leave,
go somewhere else
to put some distance
between herself
and It.

(Like me,
when she
came home
again
he would
still be
gone.)

And then,
like me,
she heard
from him.

As a small boy
on vacation
he had thrown
a bottle

with a message
he had scribbled
into the ocean.

Now, years since
he had died
and years since
they were there,
the bottle
turned up
with his message
for her:

I am here,
and I love you.
I am fine.

(Just like mine!)

July 11, 2003

Lessons from the New Sciences

It was always
a mystery
why I felt
so drawn
to the new sciences:
quantum physics
chaos,
complexity...
long before
(a decade and more)
long before
our son died
when all I wanted to do
was die, too.

Everything's connected
I always "knew."
But how?
(The Mystery.)

Ordinary miracles:
Subtle patterns,
hidden order,
ambiguity,
BOTH waves AND particles.
Paradox!
Feather floating Gump.

A lifeline from the ether,
a self-organizing (Meta) system
of support,
a circling dolphin pod
of friends unseen
I never knew
to comfort me (wow).

The Tao of Physics,
complementarity,
uncertainty, and
Schrodinger's cat.
Ah yes,
the observer.
Now what about that?

And, what "butterfly effect"
of chaos comes
with death
of one so young,
so good
as Eric?

What lifts my head
to see the stars,
the billion
spiral galaxies?

Synchronicities
and nautilus shells,
the coastline of Oregon,
meandering rivers (flying),
the veins
here in my hand,

fractal patterns
that connect
the living, loving
Universe
right here
in each of us.

Eric found!
in Consciousness!
(Or so I have observed.)

October 25, 2003

Author's Bio

Sandra J. Underwood lives in South Carolina with her husband, Richard. Married for forty-one years, both are retired from Clemson University after decades-long careers there — she, as an administrator in strategic planning and he, as an English professor and Shakespeare scholar. Living in a house on Lake Hartwell, she has written this book to help other survivors of suicide as they go through their grief and loss.

Printed in the United Kingdom
by Lightning Source UK Ltd.
101579UKS00002B/1